ADHD Heroes

JUDY BRENIS

ISBN: 1493634178
ISBN 13: 9781493634170
Library of Congress Control Number: 2013920482
CreateSpace Independent Publishing Platform
North Charleston, South Carolina

DEDICATION

This book is dedicated to my oldest daughter, who continues to fight every day to do the best that she can.

TABLE OF CONTENTS

ACKNOWLEDGMENTS

Writing this book has been an incredible journey in too many ways to list here. But I would like to acknowledge all of those who have helped me along the way, both to write the book itself and to believe in myself during the process.

Duane Gordon, editor of the Attention Deficit Disorder Association (ADDA) newsletter, my idea person! It was Duane who originally came up with the concept of a book that would tell the stories of ADHD heroes, and he has been there for me every step of the way since.

David Giwerc, founder of the ADD Coach Academy (ADDCA), who turned me on to ADHD coaching from the moment I looked at the ADDCA website. It was David who taught me how to believe in myself and how, as an ADHD coach, I could help my clients understand they are unique and not broken, and that they can create wonderful and fulfilling lives. David was also one of my "cheerleaders," whom I could always count on to build up my confidence whenever it began to wane. David's excitement and enthusiasm for this project helped me believe that writing this book was truly an important endeavor.

Mayuri Mandel, my editor and cousin, who took my words and treaded lightly with them. I am indebted to you for valuing my work, while at the same time doing what great editors do—giving wings to each and every word on the page.

Mark Brenis, my husband, who always believed that one day I would write a book, and who has patiently shared the ups and downs of this year-long process with me, letting me vent or ramble, plan or strategize, worry or exult. Thank you for being there for me.

Aryn, Sarah and Taylor Brenis, my three daughters, who told me when it was time to "get a life." I hope this book will make them proud of their mom for getting out behind the pages of someone else's book and creating my own. Love you forever and always.

Fay Taragan, my best friend for the past 50 years, who has shared life's journey with me ever since we met in first grade at Milliken Elementary School in Cleveland Heights, Ohio. Thank you for being there for me like no other.

Gert Goldman, my mom, without whom I wouldn't be the person I am today. If it weren't for you, I wouldn't have known how to create the mother/daughter relationships I have with my own daughters. I love you, mom!

And finally, thank you to all those who have placed their trust in me by allowing me to share your very personal stories with the world. I hope I have honored each and every one of you by treating your stories with love and respect.

—Judy Brenis

FOREWORD

For over 15 years, I have talked to thousands of adults diagnosed with ADHD who came to coaching or one of my many teleclasses, presentations and live seminars in the depths of despair, dogged by feelings of hopelessness, overwhelm, fear and anxiety. They eventually learned to embrace the fact that they possess a unique type of brain wiring with trillions of diverse ways of processing learning, performing and being in the world. Once they understood that having ADHD did not mean they were broken—nor had they ever been—they realized they had been participating in a game created by someone else, the rules of which did not serve them well. Once they chose to play by their own set of rules they transformed their lives, shifting their focus from problems, pessimism and procrastination to possibilities, passion and purpose. They created and are now living fulfilling lives. They pursue their unique visions with the understanding that they are not their ADHD.

Whatever you passionately picture, diligently desire and ardently act upon will magically manifest—but only when you give yourself permission to proceed. ADHD is what you have, but it is not who you are. Who you are is who you choose to be in any given moment. You have the power to create the kind of life that is aligned with the true values of your innermost self. When you discover the deeply held values of your heart and align them with the realistic and non-judgmental focus of your head, you will have the power to live the joyful, fulfilling life you truly desire.

In *ADHD Heroes,* writer and ADHD coach Judy Brenis, AAC, shares the stories of 26 inspiring people who have empowered themselves to not just accept their ADHD but use it as a catalyst for personal transformation. You will discover the emotional strengths, creativity and perseverance they developed and have utilized to accomplish their goals, even as you are inspired to adopt many of their tactics yourself.

You will learn about each ADHD hero's story of resilience in the face of adversity in order to overcome the internal and external obstacles that this condition presents. You will notice how each person embraced the natural talents and character strengths they already possessed but had buried deep inside. You will experience their personal journeys of exploration and how they learned to give themselves permission to proceed and create authentic lives full of passion, purpose and possibilities.

I know you will enjoy *ADHD Heroes* and learn as much as I have with each story. You will be inspired by the character strengths, humility, creativity and powerful purpose all these ADHD heroes manifested to transform their lives. This book will be a constant source of inspiration for adults with ADHD. It will move your heart and motivate you to take new steps toward creating the life you were meant to live!

David Giwerc, MCAC, MCC, BCC, Founder and President of the ADD Coach Academy, and author of *Permission to Proceed: The Keys to Creating a Life of Passion, Purpose and Possibility for Adults with ADHD*

Chapter 1

A CRUSADER FOR ADULT
ADHD AWARENESS

"Up to 71 percent of alcoholics, one quarter of drug abusers, and 45 percent of the prison population have this thing in common. In a woman this thing is associated with an increase in eating disorders, obesity, a higher divorce rate, seven-fold increase in unplanned pregnancies, and a doubling in the likelihood that she will take her own life. This thing affects nine million adults in the United States alone, 85 percent of whom don't know it. This thing is responsible for billions in increased medical and justice system costs, billions more in reduced business productivity—an untold personal misery every single day. This thing is ADHD in adults."
—Alan Brown, TED Talk 2012, San Diego

These days Alan Brown is a successful executive, investor, and entrepreneur. But before he became aware of his ADHD, he says that on more occasions than he can possibly recount, he came within one inch of being among the very worst-off groups of people—either in prison or dead.

"One inch of slack from the cop who knew I was dealing drugs, who knew I was committing grand larceny," Brown says. "Maybe one more inch of uncut cocaine that I might have snorted, delivering that fatal heart attack on any given day across years of abuse. But I got aware, and before I got aware I got lucky—by an inch!"

Brown describes driving from New Jersey into Harlem during the height of the crack epidemic—a conspicuously white guy in a tough black neighborhood entering an abandoned tenement building and climbing up flights of broken stairs to an apartment, in which the only things inside were a table, a scale, a block of cocaine, and a guy with a gun.

"I am the same guy as hundreds of thousands of non-violent criminals who are stuck in our prison system—the same guy as somebody who, right now, is out there unwittingly self-medicating with drugs or booze, the woman who sits depressed with suicidal thoughts," Brown says. He emphasizes again, "I just got lucky!"

In his younger years Brown was the class clown, the academic underachiever, the irresponsible space-case, the college drop-out. As an adult he experienced a failed marriage, money problems, and alcohol and drug abuse.

In elementary and middle school Brown says his grades were average, but his mom always said, "You're brighter than that."

In high school he didn't even realize that he might not graduate until the school counselor came up to him during his senior year, grabbed him by the collar, and said, "Do you understand you are not going to graduate unless you improve your grades? And you better begin ASAP!"

By that time Brown had begun drinking with his buddies, and school was not a high priority. He graduated high school by the skin of his teeth and, thanks to a few of his parents' friends who had connections, got into Seton Hall University, located in his home town of South Orange, New Jersey. Brown started out as a philosophy major, but it didn't take him long to flunk out. "I just couldn't keep up," he says.

After spending time as a musician, Brown decided at the age of 24 to return to school and major in economics. "I was interested in the subjects I was taking this time around," he says. "That helped a lot." At last his grades shot up, reflecting this interest.

However, in order to both keep up with the workload and pay for school, Brown began doing and dealing drugs. At first he simply self-medicated with cocaine and speed to deal with school, but it didn't take him long to become a cocaine addict. And although he did manage to make the dean's list a few times by using drugs as a study aid, Brown's addiction steadily took control of his life.

It took Brown ten years, but he finally graduated in 1988 with a Bachelor's Degree in Economics. After bartending for a while, Brown managed to get an entry level job at an ad agency—"the beginning of the end of my use of drugs," he says. "All of a sudden I had something to lose."

At the same time, Brown says, his mother was in the hospital dying of ovarian cancer. He remembers stopping to visit her on his way to and from Harlem to pick up drugs. "One night I realized the absurdity of the situation," he says sadly. "What kind of son would leave his dying mother's side to buy drugs?"

He picked up the phone, called 411, and said, "I need help." The operator steered him to an Alcoholics Anonymous/Narcotics Anonymous meeting, where he told his story. Brown says that the realization of not being there for his mom, coupled with his new job in the advertising world, helped him get clear of drugs and begin to focus on an industry he was very excited about.

He recalls doing fairly well and working hard, but as time went on he couldn't understand why he wasn't moving up the ladder more quickly—that is, not until he was diagnosed with ADHD at the age of 36.

Rather than causing him to look back and dwell on the negative, Brown says the diagnosis provided him with a clear and profound explanation of why his life had gone the way it had until that point. "I'm really a fairly smart, funny guy," he says, recalling his frustration about how these attributes hadn't carried him further. Suddenly, it all made sense.

The road to diagnosis wasn't easy, though. Five years previously, Brown's boss was diagnosed with ADHD following his own son's diagnosis. Hearing about the challenges that his boss struggled with, Brown thought, "That sounds like me." He went to his family doctor, who unfortunately told him, "ADHD is a myth created by the media." Brown was told to go home, work harder, and do more crossword puzzles in order to stimulate the brain. "So I went home, did more crossword puzzles, and continued to bust my butt, getting very few returns on my efforts."

Then in 1997, while sitting in a cafe reading the *Village Voice,* Brown noticed an announcement about an ADHD support group. The featured speaker was a doctor who would be talking about those in the medical profession who understood ADHD and those who didn't. Brown went to the meeting and then immediately switched doctors, finding one whose own son had ADHD. She put him through a battery of tests to rule out any physical issues, and he subsequently went to see a psychiatrist who told him he had a classic case of ADHD.

Brown began taking Ritalin, which he has continued to take for the past 17 years. He read *The Seven Spiritual Laws of Success* by Deepak Chopra, and learned how to quiet his mind and practice gratitude. Brown also began to form strategies of his own to help himself succeed.

"Within three years my career went from being an account executive, which is rather low on the totem pole, to being Vice President/ Management Director of one of the largest ad agencies in the country," Brown says proudly. He also earned Employee of the Year Award while simultaneously moonlighting for a startup he had co-founded with two partners.

Just a few months after winning this award, Brown took a leap of faith and quit his job at the advertising agency to devote all his time to the startup, which created online tools to help colleges and universities recruit and retain students. A few years later the company sold for millions of dollars.

In the meantime Brown had returned to the advertising business, where he worked for the next ten years while he continued to educate himself about his own ADHD. He recalls with amusement the day he was diagnosed and how he wandered into a bookstore and purchased a variety of ADHD-related books. When he brought them home, however, he was disappointed to see they were all text-only. "Not a single picture," he remembers with a laugh. "Small print, boring lines of type." Like many people with ADHD, sustained focus while reading is difficult for Brown, and he knew that realistically he was not going to be able to get through that pile of books.

He toyed with the idea of creating pop-up books that would provide ADDers with the ability to actually read and absorb helpful tools and strategies for coping with their ADHD. While that idea never materialized, in 2010 Brown did create ADD Crusher™ (http://www.addcrusher.com), a website featuring videos that provide interactive instruction in a fun, ADHD-friendly way.

Each video has five "ADD-crushing strategies" that take just five minute to learn and five minutes a day to practice, turning them into life-changing habits. Number one is to feed your brain. "If you go into the office having had coffee with sugar added to it, and a croissant or donut, this is sugar and simple carbs, and we know for most ADDers the mental energy from this will burn off quickly. Instead, you need to have a protein-based breakfast. Diet, exercise, and sleep habits provide a powerful foundation for escaping overwhelm and living to your potential," Brown says.

The videos also present strategies for powering up the mind and creating motivation on demand, he explains. Taking control of time, along with improving memory and organization, are among the many other coping skills presented.

Brown also encourages other adult ADDers to understand their past. "For instance, I did drugs because I was self-medicating. I committed crimes because I was seeking stimulation, and I had a willingness to do stupid things for peer approval," he points out.

"Come to terms with your ADHD," he says. "Don't regret it. See it as part of the quilt that makes up your interesting life history. You are your stories. Use your painful memories as forward-moving fuel."

Today Brown's mission is to help adults living with ADHD (nine million in the U.S. alone), including the 85 percent who remain undiagnosed and untreated, live up to their potential. He wants to reach out to those who are walking around like he used to, not understanding why they are floundering. He wants to get people talking about the fact that while the U.S. prison system ignores ADHD, prisons in other countries screen for it and achieve reduced recidivism as a result.

Brown urges everyone to go to the ADHD self-diagnosis test at PsychCentral (www.psychcentral.com/addquiz.htm) and take it. "Pass it along to someone you know who might benefit from it, post it on your Facebook page, tweet it out," he implores. "Talk about it. I'm sure everyone knows someone who is affected by ADHD."

In addition to promoting ADD Crusher™ Brown speaks at ADHD conferences and conventions around the country. He even spoke to the same support group that gave him the key to his own diagnosis years ago.

"I have never been more thrilled to be alive," Brown says. "Doing what I'm doing—to be able to work full time with ADD Crusher™, helping others. There is nothing else I can see myself doing."

Chapter 2

ADHD IS NOT A DIAGNOSIS
YOU NEED TO FEAR

"ADHD is not a diagnosis you need to fear. It's a diagnosis you need to embrace," says Rick Green, a Canadian comedian, satirist, writer, and ADDer himself.

Green is also the founder of the revolutionary website TotallyADD. com, where he uses humor and video to connect thousands of people around the world with the top experts on ADHD. It features more than 30 free videos, lively forums on every aspect of the condition, creative blog posts known as "Rick's Rants," and a shop full of ADHD resources.

"Let go of fear and take control of your life," says Green, who was not diagnosed with ADHD until adulthood. "Read as much as you can about ADHD, dance with it, explore it and forgive yourself for all the times you messed up. Your future is now wide open. You were just given a great insight into how your mind works and that opens up a world of possibilities. It is, in some ways, this grand adventure."

Green says that he doesn't know any adult diagnosed with ADHD who wishes they had never found out. Instead, they all say, "I wish I'd known sooner."

Growing up with undiagnosed ADHD was challenging, he admits. He always knew he was different. Part of that difference was the result of having two brothers who were both high achievers. The academic differences between them were apparent, Green says. "I was chugging along getting Cs, and a B, maybe even an A occasionally if I was really interested in the subject, but usually I was doing just enough to get by."

On one level, Green says his childhood was great because he grew up in Don Mills, a community in the North York district of Toronto, Canada funded by millionaire E.P. Taylor and designed as a self-supporting town consisting of living, working, and play spaces. The neighborhood was safe and low-pressure, and as a kid Green could go anywhere at any time.

School, however, was boring. "It was difficult and just something I endured. I got away with a lot of stuff just by joking and being funny. I didn't participate unless the subject was something I was interested in."

Green says he didn't fit in. He wasn't interested in sports, had terrible acne, and was shy and socially awkward. His friends were several years younger than he was, and even as a university student most of his friends were still in high school. "I was never interested in the social drama that most young people get caught up in and thought it was all rather stupid," he recalls.

"In all honesty, the world seemed a tragic mystery to me," says Green, who grew up in the '60s and '70s. "I was more interested in trying to figure out why people seemed hell-bent on killing each other over the color of a flag, and why so many people were going hungry when America is one of the richest countries in the world. The world just seemed insane to me."

In high school Green began to recognize his knack for making people laugh, and performed a comedy routine in the annual school show that was a great success. "For the first time I was being recognized and girls talked to me," he says. "It was like being hit by a lightning bolt, but the idea that I could make a living doing comedy never struck me."

In 1975 Green graduated from the University of Waterloo with a Bachelor of Science degree and landed his first job as a demonstrator at the Ontario Science Centre. While creating presentations on lasers, electricity, and cryogenics, Green developed numerous original programs, science plays, and exhibits that combined information, humor, and entertainment.

Green remembers one 75-year-old woman who came up to him after a demonstration and said, "I know nothing about science, but I understood everything you said." Green began to realize his talent for taking anything and making it understandable to anyone.

Four years later he jumped into show business full-time and helped found the Toronto-based comedy troupe The Frantics. For the next eight years he and the troupe created and performed hundreds of acts through a mix of stage shows, live appearances, 150 radio shows, several record albums, and a groundbreaking TV series.

Later Green became "Commander Rick," the writer and host of TVO's speculative fiction news magazine series "Prisoners of Gravity." At the same time he joined producer Steve Smith to co-create "The Red Green Show," writing pieces for and performing as the bumbling outdoorsman Bill for 11 seasons. The show has since spun off books (which Green co-wrote and illustrated), DVDs, CDs, and more. In addition, the series itself, edited by Green's wife Ava, remains a staple on PBS. Green now uses his "Bill" character in short comedy films on the TotallyADD.com website.

Green was formally diagnosed with ADHD in 2000, when his seventh-grade son went from the top of his class to failing and was diagnosed with the disorder. Green recalls seeing what was happening with his son and realizing, "This is me, too." (Today Green's son is a working engineer.)

Looking back to what he calls his workaholic days, Green muses, "I had so much on my plate back then. I'm interested in so many different things and as an adult with ADHD there is a constant curiosity to learn new things."

After his ADHD diagnosis, however, he began to cut back, learning how to hand off or finish certain jobs rather than trying to keep so many balls in the air at once. He began to learn how to be selective about what he chose to spend his time and energy on.

Along with Green's new understanding, though, came regret that he hadn't known about his condition sooner. "I could begin to see echoes throughout my childhood, and you don't get those years back," he says. "I began to see how worry and anxiety had consumed so much of my life, and now I realize that all that worrying doesn't change a thing."

So Green began to focus instead on what he could do to make a difference now. "And that's been a powerful practice," he says. "Ninety-nine percent of what I worried about never came true, and when bad things happened we handled it, we got through it."

Green also began taking ADHD medication, despite his earlier anti-medication stance, and realized that it was a lot better than drinking seven cans of caffeinated cola per day. He also began to cultivate a more compassionate outlook toward himself and others. He gradually stopped beating himself up over the things he didn't do well and began to focus on his strengths. These center around comedy, writing, directing, and acting—the paperwork he now leaves for others.

"There are people with ADHD who are leading very successful lives," Green says. "The difference is understanding and acceptance. I don't struggle nearly as much now that I know I have ADHD and what is going on."

In recent years Green wrote and directed the hour-long documentary, "ADD & Loving It?!" This groundbreaking film stars his friend and fellow comedian Patrick McKenna (also diagnosed with ADHD), and McKenna's wife Janis. The film won a New York Festivals Silver Award, became a hit on PBS, and earned Green the CAMH Foundation "Transforming Lives Award" for 2009. The two largest ADHD advocacy groups in America, ADDA and Children and Adults with Attention-Deficit/Hyperactivity Disorder (CHADD), have both endorsed the film.

"The documentary saves lives," Green says, relating how one man, planning to commit suicide, instead flushed the pills he was going to take down the toilet after watching the film and realizing there was hope.

In 2012 a second program, "ADD & Mastering It!," debuted on PBS as well. This program targets the specific challenges of ADHD through the use of 36 simple tools. Green and McKenna share proven strategies that they themselves employ—strategies that work with the ADHD mindset, Green explains. The program also features 20 ADHD experts offering clear advice to help others move forward with power and strength. "These are practices we have used to become successful ADHD adults. ADHD is just a different way of being," he concludes.

According to Green, about four or five percent of adults in North America fall into the ADHD spectrum, but only 15 percent of *that* percentage realize they have it. And of those who do know, only about half are doing anything about it. That's a lot of room for improvement. "But to be successful you have to know who you are," Green says emphatically. "When you know and you start dealing with it, you can create a life you absolutely love."

Chapter 3

ADHD CAN BE A BLESSING

Meredith Graf, a 19-year-old artist from New Orleans, considers ADHD to be a blessing. She is grateful for the many ideas that swirl around in her mind, for her natural ability to talk to anyone of any age, and, of course, for her artistic talent. "ADHD doesn't have to hold you back," she says emphatically.

Diagnosed as a second-grader, Graf began taking ADHD medication at the same time, and says she remembers thinking that the medication must be working because for the first time she was able to sit still in church.

"Medication doesn't cure ADHD, but gives me a handle on it," she says. "It's just another tool I can use."

Graf, who by the age of 12 was already considered a gifted artist, is extremely humble about the accolades she has already racked up, including three invitations to the White House. It was during the aftermath of Hurricane Katrina that Graf drew a picture of then-President George Bush's face and hands to acknowledge his help to New Orleans and sent it to the White House.

Bush not only wrote Graf a personal letter thanking her for her "thoughtfulness and creativity," but invited her to an African American recognition ceremony at the White House. "That first time I didn't get to meet him, but the following December I was invited to a Christmas party at the White House where I met the President and got to shake his hand," Graf says. "That was pretty cool." However, she declined an invitation to the annual White House Easter Egg Roll, she says with a giggle.

But what Graf really wants to talk about is her sophomore year in high school, when she says her life really changed. "I will never forget it," she states. "That was the year I took this really challenging history class and realized that what I was doing was not going to get me through school. I was tired of not knowing the answer whenever the teacher called on me, so one day I sat down and told myself I was going to get an A in that class."

Graf found a quiet place to study, and for the next two hours read the textbook from beginning to end and began to figure out how she was going to get through the class. "I remember someone telling me that you retain 90 percent of what you learn if you teach it to someone else, so I began teaching others. It was amazing, and from that day on I raised my hand in class every day," Graf says proudly.

She also turned to her school's new learning resource specialist, Kate Herndon, and requested additional time on tests. Herndon not only granted her a time extension but taught Graf how to take better notes, how to put her ideas together in a more cohesive way when writing essays, and the importance of peer editing.

"People can teach you skills and tools and you can choose to use them or not," Graf says. "I choose to use all my tools."

Graf attended a small private school and says that the small class size helped her as well. She also made sure that she was sitting in the front of the room in order to decrease distractions. "You really have to advocate for yourself," Graf says. "ADHD is not the problem, it is the people around you who can make it difficult."

She continues, "Honestly, I've never struggled in a subject once I've set my mind to getting an A." Graf admits, however, that it was hard for her parents to get her to sit down and study when she was younger. "I'm a pretty independent person and I have to want something to go for it. Then, once I decide to do something, I do it!"

For example, back in eighth grade, Graf, a huge animal lover, wrote a school essay on endangered species. "I have always been attracted to giving something that doesn't have a voice mine," says Graf, who didn't stop there, but contacted the U.S. Department of Wildlife and Fisheries and proposed that it initiate an endangered species poster contest.

"I wanted to give other children the opportunity to learn about endangered animals and become as passionate as I am," Graf says. "It was amazing to see that age didn't matter. The people at the U.S. Department of Fisheries and Wildlife listened to me even though I was just a kid, and it definitely became a joint project."

In fact, not only did they put Graf's idea into action, but once they discovered that Graf was quite an accomplished artist herself, they asked her to create a poster they could use as an award for the annual contest—which is now an integral part of our national Endangered Species Day.

Graf, however, envisioned something more. Instead of simply designing a poster, she decided to create a sculpture of a bald eagle sitting on top of a piece of American granite with a map of the United States made out of redwood, which would serve as a trophy for the winner. "Since the bald eagles were once endangered and came back, this is a success story as well," Graf points out.

The problem, however, was that Graf had never sculpted before. So she contacted James Vella, a world-renowned local sculptor. When he saw what she could do, he took Graf under his wing. The two worked together after school, with Vella eagerly giving of his time and talent.

Graf credits a great deal of her success to Vella, who went on to serve as her mentor, "teaching me everything I know," she says thankfully. "I know his morals, his life story, and I just hope that I can give of myself to someone the same way one day."

For a few years Graf's sculpture resided in the Ogden Museum at the University of New Orleans, where each year the poster contest winner's name would be engraved on a plaque attached to it. On May 21, 2013 (Endangered Species Day), the eagle was moved to the

National Zoo located in Washington D.C., where it will be displayed permanently.

"I met the first winner, a kindergartner, and you could see the excitement in his eyes," Graf recalls. "It was such a special experience to know what you have done is really meaningful. I am so grateful that my small voice was able to make a big impact, and I'm blessed to be able to follow through on my dreams."

When younger, Graf also painted an oil-on-canvas depiction of the Louisiana state flag with then-Representative Bobby Jindal's name, title, and the parishes he represented behind it. Jindal visited her school to accept the painting, and later Graf was recognized for her work in a resolution by the Louisiana state legislature. In 2011, Jefferson Parish officials declared March 3 to be Meredith Graf Day. "That was pretty cool," admits Graf, who says that normally she doesn't talk about her achievements, with the exception of that one.

"I honestly don't think much about what I do," Graf says humbly. "It all seems so easy for me. It's what comes naturally and makes me happy." Graf says that while working on her art, she focuses exclusively on what she is doing in the moment, which can provide a welcome relief from the usual busyness of an ADHD mind.

Recently, Graf designed the cover image for a fish and wildlife magazine. She is also working on the design of a pamphlet about dyslexia that will include tips and strategies to help those who have this disorder.

And if that isn't enough, currently Graf is working with a Memphis, Tennessee company called "Life Is Good" which works to promote confidence in young people. "My goal is to instill confidence in kids so that they grow up believing they are beautiful and they can learn to see the positive in every aspect of life," Graf says. The project she is working on involves children depicting how they view their life as "good." The children will be writing the "life is good" saying and drawing stick figures to accompany it, in order to express the positives they see in their self-images or the things that make them happy, Graf explains.

Always up for a challenge, Graf, who is now a student at Rhodes College in Memphis, is studying not only art but also writing, a subject she finds extremely difficult. "My dad told me, 'Life is always looking out for you, and art will come to you, but you can't pass up this opportunity.'"

Graf calls her father, who also has ADHD and dyslexia, her "ADHD hero." She says, "When he was younger they didn't know what ADHD was and just thought something was wrong with him. No one understood him back then, but I have always had my dad to understand me and what I'm going through."

Graf also volunteers for ADDA, to do what she can to help create greater awareness and acceptance of ADHD. "I just want to spread the word about ADHD and how it shouldn't stop anyone from achieving their dreams."

Chapter 4

LIFE IS AN ADVENTURE
THAT NEVER ENDS

"I love living life as an adventure that never ends," says Mike LoPresti, a 25-year-old college graduate, EMT, and firefighter. "I've just always known what I wanted to do and gone for it. I never let anything stand in my way."

The tall and athletically built LoPresti has a way of making it all sound easy, but in reality he was diagnosed with ADHD at age five and has had to learn how to overcome the challenges of the disorder.

"Sure, I know that there are some things that are more difficult for me to do than for others, but there are also things that come easier for me than for other people. I'm just a very optimistic person and try not to use things like my ADHD as an excuse."

LoPresti grew up in southern California and attended a private Catholic school until his teen years. "My middle name was trouble," he confesses. "My best friend, who had ADHD as well, and I—we were partners in crime."

The two young boys, LoPresti says, would "basically do anything and everything that was dangerous or involved fire." Some of their favorite activities included shooting bottle rockets and Roman candles at each other, launching model rocket motors into the sky without the rockets, bombing hills on their long boards, racing through the Santa Monica mountains on their mountain bikes, and laying duct tape in the street sticky side up so when cars ran over it, it would stick to their tires and make people think they had a flat tire.

LoPresti says he had trouble focusing in school and had way too much energy, but his mother resisted the medication route to deal with his ADHD. Instead, she helped him figure out what tools and strategies he could use that would help him be successful. Exercise was very important, and rather than going straight home after school to do his homework, LoPresti would get some exercise, play with friends, and only then head home to study. Again in the evening he would usually have sports practice of one kind or another.

LoPresti played soccer, football, and 11 straight years of baseball. He was also on his high school's varsity golf team.

Even today, LoPresti knows that exercise needs to play an important role in his life, and he works out nearly every day. "Sometimes I sit down to study and just can't focus, so I pack everything up, go to the gym, and when I come back, I'm more prepared to get something done."

LoPresti also admits to being a bit of an adrenaline junkie. "I love feeling alive, the adrenaline rush, getting my heart pumping, palms sweaty, and putting myself in situations where I feel momentarily out of our normal reality." LoPresti's favorite "escapes" include skydiving, mountain biking, body-boarding among huge waves, backpacking, cliff-jumping, competing in triathlons, rock-climbing, and motorcycle riding.

"But I've definitely calmed down with my craziness and have started to think about my future a little more now," he says.

In addition to exercise, LoPresti began taking Adderall halfway through his first quarter in college. "I had a hard time focusing for ten hours a week studying in high school, let alone the 25—35 hours a week I needed to do in college," he acknowledges.

But medication alone is not the answer, according to LoPresti. "It's a combination of ADHD medication, figuring out what works for you, and a positive attitude. Rather than see the glass half empty, I see it as half full."

LoPresti elaborates, "I'm at the point where I know what works and what doesn't work for me. I have my ear plugs and I know I need to be in a quiet environment with no distractions in front of me when studying. Index cards are a huge help. I need to write everything down. Using a white board for chemistry was the only reason I passed." LoPresti also says his mom, whom he credits with having been extremely supportive, taught him the importance of list-making. "I know what tools to use; it's just a matter of whether or not I use them."

LoPresti also talks about the positive impact his firefighter training has had on him. "I always wanted to be a firefighter, and as a young boy I was mesmerized by the big engines, the lights, and the sirens." While in high school, LoPresti was accepted into a fire cadet program with the Ventura County Fire Department, where he had the opportunity to see if this was what he really wanted to do. The answer was not only yes, but the training "really whipped me into shape both mentally and physically," LoPresti says.

"You learn how to adapt and overcome. As a firefighter, when you are given a problem, you can't say, 'We can't do this.' You have to figure out a way. So, yes, at times things get tough, and yes, there are times I don't want to do something or wonder if I can, but I just have to figure it out."

LoPresti, who graduated with a Bachelor's Degree in Kinesiology from California Polytechnic State University in San Luis Obispo, CA, in June 2013, earned his EMT certification right before his high school graduation and was hired by McCormick Ambulance that same year. "We ran all 911 calls with the L.A. County Fire Department, providing emergency medical treatment and transport."

Still working as an EMT, LoPresti attended the Oxnard College Regional Fire Academy, graduating with an Associate Degree in Fire Science and Technology. He also served as his class's president, and a month after graduation was brought on as a volunteer firefighter. Soon after, he was promoted to the position of paid call firefighter. His résumé also includes a stint with the Wildland Firefighter for Mountain Recreation and Conservation Authority, and today he is a part-time firefighter for the Five Cities Fire Authority. He is planning to go to paramedic school at some point down the road.

LoPresti admits to being very goal-oriented, always having one main goal in mind with lots of smaller goals leading up to it. He shares one example through the following story.

In high school one of LoPresti's main goals was to lose weight. Partially due to a thyroid condition, he was extremely overweight at that time. When his doctor told him he was on the borderline of developing type 2 diabetes, a disease his uncle suffered from and his grandfather had died of, LoPresti decided he had to make some major life changes. "I wasn't going to let my poor eating habits keep me from reaching my dreams. I didn't want to develop diabetes and I didn't want my weight to prevent me from being physically fit enough to become a firefighter. It wasn't about going on a diet, it was about changing my life," he says seriously.

LoPresti slowly began to eliminate unhealthy habits and replace them with healthier ones. First he cut out sodas, then sugary desserts, and finally cut down on calories in general. He eventually lost 100 pounds and has kept it off for more than six years now. "I try to eat healthy, but I don't go crazy," he says. "I still enjoy life."

LoPresti also talks about the effect that volunteer work has had on him. When he was 16, he went to Mexico with a church group to help build homes for the poor. "The houses we were building were tiny, with no insulation, no electricity. I realized I should stop complaining and getting frustrated with my struggles. My life was so easy compared to others." It is a perspective LoPresti has retained ever since.

"I never want people to feel sorry for me," he continues. "These are just my circumstances. I have a disorder, but I can work with it. Nothing comes easy in life. Don't allow yourself to feel like a victim."

"Reach for the stars," LoPresti says. "Even if you don't reach them, you have surpassed other goals along the way. If you really want something you can do it!"

He ends with a statement that seems to sum up his entire outlook on life. "Today I have the mindset that I can accomplish anything I set my mind to."

Chapter 5

CHAMPIONS IN THE MAKING

"Champions in the making" is how Dr. Ned Hallowell sees those who have been diagnosed with ADHD.

"Depending on how you use your ADHD, it can be a wonderful attribute," insists Hallowell, a child and adult psychiatrist, bestselling author, world-renowned speaker, and leading authority in the field of ADHD.

Oh, and by the way, Hallowell himself also has both ADHD and dyslexia.

He was 31 years old and near the end of his training in child psychiatry at the Massachusetts Mental Health Center in Boston when his neuropsychiatry teacher began to describe ADHD in a series of lectures. "I had one of the great 'a-ha' experiences of my life," Hallowell says.

As his teacher described children who chronically daydream, are very bright but have trouble focusing on any one subject for very long, and are energetic and impulsive, Hallowell thought, "So there is a name for what I have!" He began to read everything he could find on ADHD, and as his knowledge grew, not only did he recognize that he had it but that several members of his family probably did as well.

Hallowell felt like a boulder had been lifted from his back. "I wasn't all the names I'd been called in grade school—a daydreamer, lazy, an underachiever," he says. He realized that he had simply inherited a neurological syndrome characterized by easy distractibility, low tolerance for frustration and boredom, and a tendency toward impulsivity. He finally understood why he involuntarily tuned out of conversations for no apparent reason and why, when in grade school, he often grew angry, breaking pencils and throwing them around the room when he didn't immediately grasp a concept. He realized why it could sometimes take him up to seven attempts to read a page in a novel.

Now that Hallowell had a name for what was going on with him, he could begin to make sense of it. He could begin to forgive himself for some of his weaknesses and begin to focus on his strengths. Even though the Diagnostic and Statistical Manual of Mental Disorders of the American Psychiatric Association (the "DSM") only emphasizes the downside of ADHD, Hallowell instinctively knew firsthand that there was also a tremendous upside to the disorder.

The "deficit disorder" model is what creates the biggest problem, according to Hallowell. People with ADHD grow up thinking they are fundamentally flawed, not realizing that having it can be wonderfully rewarding as well. After all, Hallowell credits his ADHD with helping him to graduate with high honors from Harvard and Tulane Medical School, and then to return to Harvard to complete a residency in psychiatry at the Massachusetts Mental Health Center.

"My life changed," Hallowell says of his realization that he had ADHD. He knew his purpose in life was now to explain to the world that ADHD did not have to hold you back from following your dreams. In his own words, "My mission became helping people understand that ADHD does not need to cripple you, but if dealt with properly can lead you to a life of success."

Hallowell adds, "My ADHD diagnosis gave me a mission I'm still on today. I see myself not as a doctor who treats a disability, but rather as a doctor who helps people—adults and children alike—identify, develop, and celebrate their talents. That's why I love my work!"

In particular, Hallowell understands how easily the gifts of this condition are lost on children, amid negative comments from doctors, teachers, and even loving but frustrated parents—and how this sends these children down the road to feeling like failures or losers.

Hallowell speaks out on how ADHD is too often misunderstood and mislabeled as a disability. He points to how those with ADHD are also typically creative, intuitive, original, and full of positive energy. They tend to be independent thinkers. They can be persistent to the point of being stubborn, lending them a unique determination in many circumstances. ADDers are also usually quite sensitive, bighearted, and generous, and have charisma or that "special something." Hallowell says, "With the right guidance, these people can become hugely successful in their lives."

In 1996, with that belief in mind, he founded the Hallowell Center for Cognitive and Emotional Health, now headquartered in Sudbury, Massachusetts. Today there are Hallowell Centers in New York and San Francisco as well. The centers specialize in the diagnosis and treatment of ADD/ADHD. Hallowell says, "We see ADD not as a disability or a deficit, but as a trait, a way of being. Our job is to promote the positive qualities, while limiting the damage done by the negative."

He disagrees with the standard medical approach which views ADHD entirely as a disorder. "By disregarding the positive attributes, this approach often creates new serious disabilities: shame, fear, loss of hope, lowered self-esteem, and broken dreams."

Hallowell emphasizes that treatment should start with education. "You need to learn what ADD is and what it isn't. You need to understand ADD well enough to embrace it and realize that while it may be holding you back right now, in time, with the right help, it can propel you to the fulfillment of your dreams. You need to understand what a positive attribute ADD can be in your life."

Hallowell says that the next step is getting a proper diagnosis and then finding someone to work with who understands it. "Find a therapist who is highly knowledgeable and experienced working with people with ADHD and who takes a strength-based approach to change whatever it is in your life that is causing you problems. It's not just finding someone who can prescribe you medication but someone who can help you break through all the inaccurate labels and unfair judgments you have dealt with. Someone you can be open and real with and you trust completely."

Hallowell talks about the importance of not only changing how you see yourself, but getting on a regular sleep schedule and building exercise into your life. You also need to value the importance of healthy eating, and then perhaps even move on to reconsider your job or school situation in light of your ADHD. Various structural changes can make a big difference, insists Hallowell—such as the right filing system, organizational strategies, and daily schedule.

In addition to education, coaching, and therapy, Hallowell says that the key to creating a successful life with ADHD is developing your talents and interests. "You build a life not on weaknesses you have repaired, but on talents you have developed."

Hallowell often says that having ADHD is like having a powerful race car for a brain, but with bicycle brakes. "Treating ADHD is like strengthening your brakes, so rather than crashing into walls, you start to win races in your life."

*   *   *

Dr. Hallowell was a member of the Harvard Medical School faculty from 1983 to 2004. Among the many books that he has authored or co-authored on various psychological topics are *Driven to Distraction* and *Delivered from Distraction,* both on life with ADHD. He also speaks all over the world and has appeared on CNN, PBS, NPR, 20/20, "The Oprah Winfrey Show", "60 Minutes" and "The Today Show," among others.

Chapter 6

DO WHAT MAKES YOU HAPPY

At the age of 32 Michael Camoin was fired from his job as a school social worker, then diagnosed with both ADHD and depression.

Eighteen years later he is a leader in independent film production in northeastern New York and co-founder of Upstate Independents, Inc., a network for the Association of Independent Video and Filmmakers established in 1995 and now home to more than 200 media artists.

"My passion is pursuing independent motion pictures—and I rarely ever look at the clock other than to see how much time is left in the day," says Camoin, whose road to success began once he let go of doing what he thought he *should* do and decided to build upon his love of independent films, a dream he'd had since he was a very young boy.

"My brother and I would take our father's 8mm film projector, close the garage door, and drape a sheet over it. We'd charge the neighborhood kids a nickel to watch these short films we had collected and kept in a shoebox," Camoin says.

But like so many people with ADHD, Camoin got sidetracked along the way. An English major, he ended up working as a camp counselor and computer salesman before returning to college to earn a Master's Degree in Social Work. This time he did land a job in his chosen field, and was hired as a school social worker. Six years later, however, he was refused tenure. "When I didn't receive tenure, I finally thought, 'Boy, there has to be a reason for this,'" says Camoin. This blow to his career was the catalyst that caused him to seek help from a therapist, which led to his diagnosis of ADHD and depression.

"Getting diagnosed was actually a relief," Camoin says. "Knowing why I had struggled so much helped me understand it wasn't my fault." Armed with this new understanding of himself, Camoin began to read and learn about his ADHD, also hiring an ADHD coach to help him create tools and strategies "to help me handle and manage my ADHD symptoms."

David Giwerc, ADHD coach and founder of the ADD Coach Academy, worked with Camoin. They focused on simple things that made a huge difference, such as always hanging his keys on a hook be-hind the door so that he no longer had to worry about where they were or spend time looking for them. They also worked on the big things; Giwerc helped Camoin develop ways to rein in rumination, negative thoughts, and impulsivity. Camoin shares an example: "Today I know not to hit that 'send' button after writing an e-mail if I'm upset. I wait until I have run it by others."

Giwerc also gave him some very good words of advice—focus on the things you are passionate about. Do what makes you happy.

Having already moonlighted as a film director for six years, Camoin heeded this advice and applied for a loan through the Americans with Disabilities Act to create his own video production company. "My coach taught me to look at my assets and how ADHD can be an added benefit, not a deficit," Camoin says. "When I take a good look at my-self, I see that I really have extraordinary abilities, abilities that most people don't have."

"Sure there are challenges," he says, but when they arise Camoin now knows he can figure out a way around them instead of giving up. For example, when he discovered that ADHD medication did not seem to help him, he and his coach figured out that exercise, which releas-es serotonin, helped tremendously with getting his brain in gear and ready to work. So exercise became a regular part of his daily schedule.

"When I wanted to write a screenplay, a dream I've had for a very long time, I'd get on my bike, my laptop in my backpack, and ride, stopping on the way home at a local café," Camoin says. "There I would put on my headphones, listen to music, and begin to type. Next thing you know, 30 days later I had written a 95-page screenplay."

Camoin also began to give himself permission to delegate the tasks he finds difficult, such as bookkeeping and other paperwork. By hiring interns, he not only reduces his workload and stress level, but finds it extremely satisfying to help others who want to break into the film industry. "There is nothing better than when someone comes back to thank me for giving them their first paying job in the industry. That's cool," Camoin says.

"And it gives me time to do what I do best, creating. I love everything about film. Filmmaking and storytelling are my passion. I love to do it, and even when I'm not getting paid to do it, I do it. At the end of the day, when you're in the editing room and you put things together that were meant to be together, two scenes that just go together, that's so wild," Camoin enthuses.

"To be a director you need to understand history, music, painting, business, and economics. I love being involved in every aspect of it. It seems endless to me, from the writing stage to the incredible challenge of finding financing, envisioning the end result, reaching the audience, and knowing beforehand that it is going to have an emotional impact on the people viewing it."

Camoin emphasizes that people with ADHD shouldn't let it hold them back. "First learn about your ADHD. Read about it to better understand yourself and how it impacts you. A big part of managing it is becoming more self-aware. As someone with ADHD, you are extra-sensitive. You are attuned to a lot of things, but you might not be attuned to yourself. Get a support system in your life. Find an ADHD coach who has an interest in your field of business, a coach with whom you feel a connection."

Camoin continues, "I've met hundreds of creative professionals who are suffering needlessly; they're hindering their own careers as writers, musicians, and artists. They're extremely bright, yet completely un-aware of the skills needed to manage their ADHD traits, and there-fore they underperform. Having knowledge of ADHD and the skills to manage my symptoms keeps me grounded, focused, and on track.

"My coach always told me to remember that the good opinions of other people are not better than my own good opinion of myself. I didn't quite understand it at the time, but I came to realize that I know just as much as others. You need to respect yourself, to value your own opinion, and then become an advocate for yourself and the work you are trying to do."

Chapter 7

WITH LOVE, TO ADHD MOMS!

"**M**om, can you pick me up after school?"

"Mom, you need to fill out this paperwork!"

"Mom, what are we having for dinner?"

"Mom, I need help with my science project!"

"Mom, have you done the laundry?"

"Mom, did you sign me up for summer camp?"

Being a mother is not easy. Add ADHD to the mix, and motherhood becomes more than just a challenge. It stirs up old feelings of self-doubt, overwhelm, and anxiety. You're constantly forgetting things, you have difficulty with decision-making, planning, and follow-through—and you have to deal with an entire family in addition to all that, which just adds to the stress.

Trying to balance a personal life and family life is incredibly hard. And the guilt is endless! Not to mention the not-infrequent resentment. If you're a mother with ADHD, you probably feel that daily life is just too complicated, and you wonder when you get *your* chance to relax, socialize with friends, and enjoy life. Then, of course, you feel guilty about feeling resentful. Sometimes it seems like a no-win situation.

For Sheryl Greenfield, who was not diagnosed with ADHD until after her seven-year-old son's diagnosis, it was all about trying to stay on top of everything and never understanding why she couldn't. "I kept thinking that I needed to be that superwoman," she says. "I needed to do it all. But of course, I hadn't recognized the limitations of my executive functioning systems. I could never keep up and didn't know why."

Greenfield also harbored feelings of inadequacy and self-hate because she didn't know that ADHD affects a person's level of interest. "I often found myself bored staying home with my children," Greenfield says. "There was a lot of guilt around that."

Sharon Brown, another mother with ADHD, talks about how on the surface she appears to be just like any other "normal" mom with a "normal" child. But, she admits, "Every day I struggle with the ins and outs of daily life and parenthood that others, especially other moms, seem to breeze through effortlessly." She admits that because of the stigma of ADHD, she tries to hide her struggles—how much harder it is and how much longer it takes for her to accomplish everything.

At the same time, however, Brown acknowledges that there are other moms carrying much heavier loads than hers—and this just adds to her guilt. "I try not to complain and just continue to try to cover up my struggles. But all of this makes me feel alone, confused, anxious, depressed, and often inadequate and misunderstood."

Brown and Greenfield are certainly not alone. Many women, particularly those with ADHD, also feel shame when the cultural messages that women receive are instructions to be nice, help others, don't say no, don't ask for too much, and don't hurt anyone's feelings.

In her book *Women with Attention Deficit Disorder* author Sari Solden (whom you'll also meet later, in Chapter 12) writes, "For women with ADHD these cultural messages can have an even greater impact, creating an internalized sense of self-blame, of not being good enough. It is essential for them to confront these messages in order to create the necessary changes to make their lives work for them." Solden points out that these changes have to be made at home, at school, in women's jobs, and in their relationships.

Mothers with ADHD also tend to put their own needs at the bottom of the list, and because it takes them longer to get things done, those needs never get met. For author and mother Cathy Riehl, for example, writing gives her great joy and a sense of peace. "I have no trouble focusing when I'm writing," she says. "And when I'm done, I feel rejuvenated." Yet she rarely finds the time to get into her studio to write because she feels that she has to take care of her family first.

Having a child with ADHD creates another layer of self-blame, Greenfield says. Raising her ADHD son forced her to look at herself in the mirror every day, and at first she didn't have the tolerance for that. Advocating for her son, however, became much easier, and you can hear the pride in her voice when she talks about how important it was for her to stand up for him and get him the accommodations that he needed in order to succeed.

An ADHD coach now, Greenfield says she has learned so much about her own ADHD that she can finally appreciate the upside of being a mother with this condition. She says it makes her better able to accept her son's unique talents and allow him to grow, "to let him do his own thing without getting in the way." Greenfield is proud that her son has learned how to manage his ADHD and use it to make himself shine.

Brown agrees. Having ADHD herself gives her the ability to understand her nine-year-old ADHD son—this is, in fact, one of the reasons she is working with an ADHD coach herself. She wants to be a role model for her son and show him how he can overcome the challenges of ADHD. On good days she can also look at some of her own ADHD traits, such as her creativity and intuition, as blessings and great assets to have when parenting. "My creativity and intuition help me to be more resourceful," she says. "To let go of things and have more fun, especially at homework time with my son."

Both Greenfield and Brown encourage mothers with ADHD to find or establish support systems for themselves. "And I'm talking multi-model," Greenfield says. "It's not just going to a support group, not just taking a pill thinking that is going to manage your ADHD. It means going to someone who knows what you are talking about, building up your self-esteem. You need a support *team,*" she insists. "Work with a psychiatrist who knows how to handle your medication, a therapist who understands ADHD, and an ADHD coach."

Brown adds, "I love my coach because she really understands ADHD, and therefore I get better results from our sessions and especially out of myself. It's very empowering." She also says it is so important for mothers with ADHD to focus on the basics of wellness, including a healthy diet, good sleep, exercise, and spiritual nourishment. She also suggests that ADHD moms discover the ways they learn best. "Are you a visual, auditory, or kinesthetic learner? Once you know your strengths you have more options to thrive."

Brown insists, "And lastly, don't give in to the chatter in your head. Re-program yourself with self-love."

Just like the old African proverb says, it takes a village to raise a child.

And it also takes a support team to help turn the challenges of ADHD into strengths.

Here are some tips for mothers dealing with ADHD on top of their families:

- Take care of yourself. Exercise, get adequate sleep, and be sure to eat well.

- Simplify. This applies to meals, housework, and clothing options. Along with anything else you can make simpler and easier.

- Create a family calendar. This helps keep everyone's commitments in full view at all times.

- Clarify household rules. Write them down and post them where everyone can see them.

- <u>Get help</u>. Find solutions to problems by enlisting the help of your friends and family.

- <u>Beat the morning rush</u>. Make a list of what needs to be done in the morning the night before. Leave everything you will need to take with you by the front door. Have your children do the same.

- <u>Remember that it's not *your* homework</u>. When your kids honestly do need help with it, don't be afraid to enlist others—friends, other family members, even tutors if necessary.

- <u>Don't over-volunteer</u>. Resist the temptation to help others before you help yourself.

- <u>Do not neglect your own needs</u>. This above all! Taking care of yourself first ensures you'll be more available to others—and you'll be happier for it, too.

Chapter 8

OF COURSE I CAN, ONE NOTE AT A TIME

"**O**nce you stop looking at what you can't do because of your ADHD and start focusing on what you *can* do, you can make your dreams come true," says Josh Greenfield, a 27-year-old musician and up-and-coming foodie.

"I used to think I wasn't good at anything, but once I began to question that belief, I realized I had only convinced myself I wasn't good enough," Greenfield says. "I'm actually good at music and cooking and as soon as I gave myself permission to believe that and follow my passion, everything began to fall into place."

Today Greenfield performs with the band Canon Logic and runs a catering company with his younger brother, Mike. The two brothers also host their own cooking show called "The Brothers Green," which can be found on the Hungry Channel.

"Both music and food help us connect with people," says Greenfield, who felt very isolated growing up. Diagnosed with ADHD in elementary school, Greenfield began taking Ritalin in third grade and while it helped him focus, he felt he lost his personality. He felt as if he was in a bubble, only concerned with getting his homework done and focusing on school. "Teachers thought I was this golden child until last period when the meds began to wear off."

College started out the same way, until Greenfield decided to stop taking medication. Before long he was focusing on his music more than his studies. "I got good grades to appease my parents since they were paying for college, but I would rather be home writing songs. At the end of the day, nothing makes me feel the way playing music does."

"Growing up I was always told I had a learning disability. I didn't know what that meant, but I was in special classes. My mom was trying to figure out what to do with me. That puts up a lot of walls. It really isolates you from the rest of the world," Greenfield explains.

"I wasn't sure if I was stupid, if I would ever be able to focus, to read a book. I thought I couldn't pay attention to anything, but when I started playing guitar, I was practicing eight hours a day and it was great. I thought, 'Wait a minute, I can focus on this!' Suddenly, I didn't feel like I had a learning disability, and I realized I was never told I could succeed."

In fact, Greenfield's music career almost never got off the ground because he lacked confidence. Back in middle school, Greenfield attended a party with his parents and remembers being mesmerized by the band playing there. "I was just really intrigued by it," he says. He remembers the bass player handing him his guitar and "when I hit the strings I was just amazed. I thought, this is incredible!" But when Greenfield asked his parents for a guitar and began taking lessons, he was surprised by how difficult it was to play and immediately quit.

He didn't pick up a guitar again until the summer between his freshman and sophomore years in college. His girlfriend travelled to Costa Rica while he went to study in Michigan, and a chance meeting there rekindled his love of playing. "I met this guy staying in the dorm room next to mine who could play every single Dave Matthews song," says Greenfield. This was the perfect opportunity to learn a catalogue of great songs his girlfriend would appreciate when she returned from her trip, he reasoned, because she was a huge Dave Matthews fan. "For six straight weeks, all I did was play the guitar."

And the rest, as they say, is history.

The following school year, in 2005, Canon Logic was born. "At the time we were just two guys writing music, recording on a small machine and putting out music for free on the Internet," Greenfield said. "Anyone who liked the music could download all of it for nothing, and if they wrote to us, we would either write a song about them or let them help us design artwork. We were very hands-on with the few fans we had, and formed close connections to some great people from all around the country. Over the years, through the Internet mostly, we found other band-mates who enjoyed the music we were making and wanted to be a part of what we were doing."

Today, Canon Logic plays all over the East Coast, and recently the company Shutterfly began using a song the band recorded a few years ago in one of its holiday commercials.

Despite his preoccupation with music, Greenfield did graduate from the University of Delaware with a degree in marketing, but then he moved to New York and ended up working as a private investigator. It was while spending long hours just sitting in his car that Greenfield began to read about Buddhism and began journaling. He says he began to really work on himself, studying how to condition the mind and body to create more balance in his life. "The concepts are really quite simple," he says. "I realized I had already been feeling this way but I hadn't known how to implement those beliefs. Once I had the steps, it really became a beautiful thing."

One of the most important lessons Greenfield took from his studies of the ancient religion of Buddhism was what the Buddha said regarding the path to enlightenment. According to Greenfield, the Buddha advised his followers to use his teachings as a raft to get you from one side of the river to the other. "But once you have made it across, do not carry the raft on your back for it will only weigh you down. Release the raft and live your life."

"So that's what I began to do," Greenfield says. "That's when I began to focus on all I could do. I realized I see my true abilities when I'm excited about things. Often, when people are searching for truth and inner peace they get caught up in the head games, in the teachings, in the knowledge that exists outside of them, outside of that very moment. They think too much about lessons and teachings; at some point, if they really want to feel free, they have to simply let go."

But music isn't Greenfield's only passion. He also loves to cook, and in 2009 when he was laid off from his private investigator job due to the recession, he started cooking most of his meals. "I invited lots of friends over, mostly struggling artists who loved food but had little money, and I was cooking for them all the time.

"Word slowly spread about my love of food and my ability to cook for people; soon I was delivering weekly meals to peoples' doorsteps, cooking for private dinner parties, and offering cooking lessons. Before I knew it, I was delivering eight customers weekly meals packed up in Tupperware and I was finding ways to pay the rent."

Greenfield says his interest in cooking actually began when he was much younger and still taking ADHD medication. While he didn't have much of an appetite due to the Ritalin, Greenfield said he would tune into the cooking show "Emeril Live" late at night and that alone seemed to quench his appetite. Then a funny thing happened. The summer before Greenfield's senior year, his girlfriend invited him to join her and her family at their beach house, a beautiful home on the Jersey Shore where they had a chef who prepared all the meals.

Greenfield said he couldn't believe his luck when he found out the chef had grown up with, and later trained with Emeril Lagasse himself. "So I just began helping him out, and this guy treated me like a student rather than a houseguest. Every morning I would help him prep for the day, and that really inspired me."

Greenfield's passion for food only grew and before long he invited his brother Mike, who had just graduated from college with a degree in architecture, to move in and join him in the business. "He really helped the business grow into something real," Greenfield says. "At the time I was calling us 'Food Wheelers,' since we were wheeling-and-dealing food to friends in need all over New York City in a way that others had yet to explore. When a new roommate who was a film maker moved in, he started documenting what we did, all the parties we threw, all of the food that surrounded us and we started cutting up the footage and releasing edits under the name YuNork. Slowly the whole dynamic shifted from just cooking to being on camera. He would even have us play our music while grilling on the roof."

Someone from the "Rachael Ray" show heard about the Greenfield brothers and in 2011 invited them to appear on a show competing against each other in a burger cookout with Nick Jonas as judge. Before long "Brothers Green" was born on YouTube, and after a year of presenting a rather traditional cooking show, they were given free rein to create their own style, complete with a budget and their own film crew.

Today Josh and Mike face a culinary challenge in every episode and focus on taking everyday ingredients and combining them in very unusual ways. The show is filmed from their home loft kitchen in Brooklyn, New York, and reveals the camaraderie and love the two brothers have for each other in addition to their cooking skills and creativity.

Music and food connect Greenfield with others. "I like to make people happy, to inspire them. It's a way to bring everyone together. That has always been in the forefront of everything I do," he says. "Even before I was playing, I was dancing. I like to get people up and moving. Music and food are universal languages. They are the two things that everyone has some form of connection to."

He continues, "Food plays such an important role in everyone's life. It determines how we feel, our energy levels, our mood. Using food as a vehicle to understand yourself, to understand your body, to understand what makes you feel good is an important part of my life, and I am drawn to sharing that with the world."

Greenfield emphasizes eating healthy and says, "It's not about losing 30 pounds in two weeks; it's about changing habits slowly and realizing how much that can change your life. If you're willing to put in the time, to really focus, that's when real change happens. It's not about overnight success. It's about working slowly and confidently. Sure, you may fail once, twice, three or four times, but eventually you create positive change."

As an ADDer, Greenfield knows what it's like to wonder if you are up for challenges, but after taking the leap he doesn't really think about his ADHD other than as a way to help him understand himself and to use what he has learned from it to his advantage. "Now I have no trouble focusing," he says. "I work all the time and have learned so many different things. Now it's very rare that I think I can't do something, and that feeling only lasts a minute, because I quickly realize, 'Of course I can!'"

Chapter 9

CREATING ADHD AWARENESS IN THE BUSINESS WORLD

Jay Carter's resume reads like an entry from *Who's Who in Business,* but that wasn't always the case. He shares that his psychologist once said, "Jay Carter has taken a rather circuitous route to his present success."

"That couldn't be truer," agrees Carter, who has worked at the same Fortune 100 company for the past 14 years despite his ADHD.

Labeled a troublemaker as a child, Carter could never quite figure out how he ended up in the principal's office or in yet another fight. "I never set out to get myself in those kinds of situations," he says.

Carter came from a typical working family, with his dad a lawyer and his mom a nurse. His grades were pretty good in elementary school because he didn't have to try very hard, but at parent-teacher conferences a different story would emerge. The teachers always told his parents that Jay was a delightful child, and things would be fine . . . if only he would stop fighting and keep his mouth shut.

Inconsistency was the only constant in Carter's years at school. His grades were erratic, totally dependent on his interest in a given subject. In high school he felt very isolated, an emotion fed by some of the situations that had occurred in elementary school. He tried attending boarding school, but returned to high school again after being kicked out. This time Carter excelled, skipping his senior year and then attending a branch of Emory University—where, of course, everything fell apart. "I did pretty well my first two terms, but then I was dismissed for missing too many classes."

Carter also admits to a fairly common experience of people with ADHD—he spent a year in rehab. "If you understand ADHD, there's a lot of self-medicating related to it and the baggage you pick up living a life that's out of control," he explains.

After rehab Carter bounced from one job to another, either quitting or being fired. At age 25, however, he began to turn his life around. First, he says, he "married the right woman." Then he finally got serious about school. "One of the big differences for me was that when I went back, I went to school full-time and worked full-time. Even now I find I do much better when I'm busy. School by itself provided too much free time. So I made myself busy enough that I couldn't mess around, and that helped focus my attention."

A bit older than his fellow students, Carter further differentiated himself by majoring in international business and German. He and his wife then moved to Germany during his junior year, where he attended the University of Heidelberg. This was followed by a year at the University of Trier, also in Germany, where he studied finance and strategic management.

Upon graduation, Carter served as a German language interpreter at the 1996 Summer Olympic Games in Athens, Georgia. "That opened a lot of doors and gave me a great deal of confidence," he says. He then went to work for the German airline Lufthansa. Following this, he again went back to school to earn his MBA while working full-time, receiving mostly straight A's with just one B in his classes. "It really is amazing when you remember how erratic my grades were earlier," Carter says. "It's part of the paradox of ADHD, but it also gives people hope when they see that you can have ADHD and still focus long enough to get an MBA or get through school."

In the midst of all of this, Carter and his wife began their family. They now have three children (15, 13 and 5 years old); two have been diagnosed with ADHD. It was only while researching his daughter's learning challenges that Carter read *Driven to Distraction* by Edward Hallowell and John Ratey. "On every page there was something I could relate to," he says.

He visited a local assessment center in Chicago, where he was living at the time, and was officially diagnosed. He began taking ADHD medication, and upon moving back to Minnesota to work at a different job in the same company, "a job that was a much better fit," he began seeing a psychologist. Carter attended ADHD support group meetings as well, and it was there that he met the person who would become his ADHD coach.

In 2008 Carter took an even bolder step when, in an effort to help provide publicity for an ADHD awareness conference that was going to take place in his town, he contacted the local newspaper and spent hours being interviewed about his ADHD. Carter says he wasn't that nervous about disclosing his diagnosis. "I had decided it was the right thing to do. I also thought my company would be supportive enough that the disclosure wouldn't be an issue, and it really hasn't been."

Carter admits he is very lucky that his employer understands, but he is quick to assure others that in most cases, people with disabilities can get what they need to be more productive without disclosing everything. "I tell people to disclose to the extent that they need to, in order to get what they need." Carter says, for example, that you can tell your employer you 'have trouble concentrating,' or simply ask your boss to give you a list of tasks in order of priority so you will know what to work on first.

"Unfortunately there's still a stigma around the ADHD diagnosis because people don't understand it. It's a challenge we are working through. The same thing applies to some other disabilities as well, but with ADHD, a lot of the symptoms look like the things lazy people do, so there's almost a moral judgment by people who don't understand."

While accommodations can help people with ADHD be more productive at work—Carter uses speech-recognition and mind-mapping
software and receives administrative help from a virtual assistant—he
also points out how poor social skills, rather than poor productivity,
often hold back people with ADHD. He admits this was one of his biggest challenges.

"Most people don't realize what the lack of good social skills means
in a work situation. I was never comfortable with classic networking,"
Carter says. "I wasn't really good at communicating. I didn't commu-
nicate what I was doing, so people didn't realize the contribution I was
making, and for my first 12 years with the company that really had a
negative impact." Carter says he also had to learn how to stop saying
dumb things in meetings. "I did it too often; I could recognize that, but
I just couldn't stop myself."

Since being diagnosed with ADHD and working with a coach, however, Carter has made tremendous strides in his career, even receiving
a promotion despite the state of the economy. "The piece I was missing
was the understanding of my ADHD, how it manifests itself and how
it impacts my life," Carter says. "And one of the biggest breakthroughs
I had with my coach was re-examining the beliefs I had picked up like
tumbleweeds that had blown through my life. As an ADDer, I'm a poor
self-observer; one of the great things about coaches is how they can
stand back, reflect, and witness from an objective standpoint. I have
been able to change many of my beliefs because of this type of feed-
back, and there have been many positive results from that."

In fact, Carter is now a certified ADHD coach himself and runs
Hyperfocused Coaching Systems, LLC. "The training taught me a lot
about my own ADHD, and I really wanted to help others and have the
same kind of impact on others that my coach had on me."

Carter speaks to organizations about success in the workplace
with ADHD, and also hosts *The ADHD Weekly Podcast* at http://www.
adhdweekly.com. "I like to share what I'm learning as I go along in life.
I let people know what works for me and what might work for them,
too."

"I also like to help people unfamiliar with ADHD understand what a struggle it really is and that it's a serious condition. As ADDers sometimes we have a hard time believing how much our ADHD impacts us, ourselves," Carter says, "especially when we have gone through years of undiagnosed ADHD. Coaches can help us change our limiting beliefs."

"I wouldn't trade my ADHD for anything. It's a part of who I am," says Carter. "There really is an aspect of giftedness to it, and if I can focus 99% on my strengths and keep my weaknesses from tripping me up, that's great."

Chapter 10

DEVOTED TO SERVING THE ADHD, ASPERGER'S, AND SPECIAL NEEDS COMMUNITY

Growing up with undiagnosed ADHD, Pam Milazzo went through life thinking that she was an imposter. In law school she believed that if people just scratched beneath the surface they would see she was a "screw-up," someone who never lived up to her true potential.

"I felt like I had people fooled and that I wasn't really who everyone thought I was," Milazzo says today.

"Although my parents made it clear to me that I tested with a very high IQ in grade school, I didn't always get the best grades. I was a solid B student, with some As and some Cs depending on my level of interest in the class, primarily because I didn't study or do my homework."

Milazzo remembers that when she was in the eighth grade she decided she wanted to get better grades, and got the bright idea that she could do that by staying up all night studying for tests. "I tried this out on a history test I had to prepare for and I walked away with a solid A on that test."

As a result, procrastination and last-minute preparation became Milazzo's best friends. Using this strategy, she was able to coast through most of her courses while doing the bare minimum amount of work. "In all honesty, I felt it was a waste of my time to start work on anything until the last minute because I couldn't get myself going until then."

Milazzo admits that college was just a repetition of high school, with more of the same approach to academics. "I literally would start the research for a term paper the day before it was due, finishing the paper five minutes before I had to turn it in. Oftentimes I didn't crack open a book until it was the night before midterms."

For the most part she received good grades, and the cycle would continue. "Unfortunately, my strategy didn't always work—in fact, I failed a couple of classes my senior year of college and had to return to school after my student teaching semester."

Not diagnosed with ADHD until she was in her 40s, however, Milazzo still didn't know that she had executive functioning challenges and that it was nearly impossible for her to focus until the last minute. This is what would create the adrenaline rush she needed in order to do her work. What she did know was that she experienced guilt—"a *lot* of it."

Milazzo graduated with a Bachelor of Science in Education from Central Michigan University and taught for four years in the inner city of Detroit. As a home economics teacher she didn't have a lot of the paperwork that many of the other teachers had, so that made it much easier for her.

Teaching English one year, however, proved a lot more challeng-ing, as did teaching fifth grade another year. "That was excruciating," Milazzo recalls. "All of a sudden I had all these different subjects to teach with little guidance from the administration. There was no struc-ture, and this just fed into all of my executive functioning challenges."

She still loved being a teacher, but due to administrative issues she felt that if she could no longer be there for her students, then she didn't belong in teaching. It was then that she had an ADHD moment. When a friend (who knew that she had once worked as a receptionist at a law firm) asked her if she had ever considered a career in law, the next thing Milazzo knew she was researching the LSAT and law schools.

Milazzo laughs at her "very ADHD decision," but her law degree proved extremely beneficial years later while advocating for her son (who was born with high-functioning autism), as well as in her advocacy as an ADHD coach.

But during the time she spent in law school actually earning that degree, Milazzo was finally faced with the fact that her old study habits wouldn't work. "I quickly learned that you had to keep up all along. There was no way you could procrastinate until the last minute. You had to be doing your work every single day."

She began leaving her apartment Mondays through Fridays and walking to the law library, where she would use one of the individual study rooms. "I didn't want people to see how I had to study. I was embarrassed. In order to complete all my work, I had to be able to move around, read out loud, and highlight everything in multiple colors," she explains. "Sitting for long periods of time was excruciating."

While procrastinating was no longer an option, Milazzo does remember once staying up for 72 hours in order to complete a brief. "But once I made it through my first year, the rest wasn't as bad," she says, adding that study groups helped her tremendously. Also vital was learning the importance of taking breaks rather than running a studying marathon, so to speak.

Milazzo earned her Juris Doctorate degree from Wayne State University Law School in Detroit and practiced law in New Jersey from 1988 through 1995, during which time she was a solo family law practitioner.

Still undiagnosed, however, Milazzo was managing because both she and her husband worked at home and her husband took care of a lot of the household responsibilities. Sadly, he passed away when her two children were very young, but even then with the help of a nanny, followed by an au pair and a housekeeper, she kept it together.

It was when she remarried that everything finally fell apart. Her new husband worked outside the home and no longer did she have the help of a nanny or housekeeper. "All of a sudden I was the one responsible for paying the bills, taking care of the house and the meals," Milazzo says. "It just became an executive functioning nightmare!"

"I felt like I was no longer employable. I had taught home economics and now could not even take care of my own home. I didn't want anyone to come to my house. It was just too embarrassing."

Milazzo became so sick that she couldn't even leave the house without someone accompanying her. In retrospect, she attributes her illness to the level of stress she was under, having placed the bar so high. She has since learned how to set more realistic expectations for herself in terms of how much she can take on.

In the meantime her daughter, who had been diagnosed with ADHD, was in the fourth grade and struggling. "She was very unorganized and her teachers were telling me that I had to help her, and I'm thinking, 'I can't even get myself organized.'"

"I decided I had to find an ADHD coach for her, and in my mind in order to do that I had to go to the ADDA conference," says Milazzo, who still didn't have a clue that she herself had ADHD as well. That is, until the next-to-last day of the conference, when she was sitting in a seminar presented by clinical psychology professor Russell Ramsey. "He began talking about wiggling your toes to help you fall asleep, and all of a sudden it all fell into place. I remember waiting to talk to Ramsey after the session and I just began crying."

Milazzo says that meeting David Giwerc, founder of the ADD Coach Academy, at this conference was also a pivotal moment for her. She signed up on the spot to become an ADHD coach—"another classic impulsive decision," she laughs, but one she doesn't regret.

After the conference Milazzo went home, got herself checked out, and was officially diagnosed with ADHD. She then found herself dealing with the grief around the belief that if she had been diagnosed as a child, she would have been able to break through all the shame and self-loathing and get the support and strategies that she would have needed in order to live up to her potential at a much earlier stage in her life.

Giwerc helped her rebuild her self-esteem, leading her to acknowledge her past accomplishments, and today Milazzo has created a very successful ADHD coaching practice. She is also devoted to serving the ADHD, Asperger's, and special needs community in a variety of ways. She is a national speaker, giving presentations and in-service training workshops throughout the country to parent advocacy groups, support groups, educators, and professionals working with the ADHD community.

Milazzo has also been a featured speaker at the CHADD national conference as well as the ADDA national conference. She previously served as Chairman of the National ADHD Awareness Campaign for ADDA and as a chapter coordinator and support group leader for the Union County New Jersey Chapter of CHADD.

As both a parent of children with learning differences and an adult with ADHD herself, Milazzo is acutely aware of the debilitating challenges, struggle, and agony parents endure in their efforts to obtain necessary services and support for their children. She not only guides families through the educational system, but works with them as she coaches their children.

Currently Milazzo is working on a program that will help her teach others how she works with the entire family. She wants to pass down all that she has learned throughout the years and help others who really want to make a difference in the world.

"For me, having the right people believe in me and show me support when I needed it has made all the difference," she relates. "It's because of their support that I was able to continue to push forward and keep trying despite my challenges."

While medication can be an important piece of the puzzle, she counsels, "your ADHD is not going to go away with a pill. It's really about understanding that this is the brain you have, and you have to work with it. You have to understand it and stop fighting it, stop looking at it from the perspective that this is some horrible thing you want to cover up."

Milazzo encourages others to seriously consider the coaching process, to take advantage of the tremendous wealth of good books now available on ADHD, and to look into local support groups to prevent feelings of isolation. "It helps to recognize that there are other people out there who have been through and/or are going through similar situations. You can recognize that there is still hope. I don't care how old you are. There is no reason to give up."

Chapter 11

PASSION WITHOUT PURPOSE IS LIKE A PERSON WITHOUT A HEART

"**M**y ADHD diagnosis changed my life," said David Giwerc, founder and president of the ADD Coach Academy (ADDCA) and author of *Permission to Proceed: The Keys to Creating a Life of Passion, Purpose and Possibility for Adults with ADHD.*

"Once I put a name to my problems of attention, interest, and hyperactivity, it freed me to explore new ways of living and being in the world, ways of being that supported my unique brain wiring," Giwerc explains. "Most importantly, once I learned how to focus on my strengths rather than my weaknesses, I could move forward."

Giwerc was not diagnosed with ADHD until the age of 38, and faced many challenges growing up. However, he says that his parents and grandparents never made him feel like a failure, and always loved and supported him. "My grandmother never let me look at my weaknesses and feel sorry for myself. She emphasized my strengths and acknowledged me every day for the things I did well."

There is a reason why he calls out his grandmother in particular. When she realized that her grandson David was unable to stop moving, she bought him a sturdy rocking chair that he still has to this day. "By the age of seven I had broken two couches, one at my grandmother's house and one at my own, as a result of rocking back and forth so violently while watching television," Giwerc remembers. "Looking back, I now realize that rocking helped me focus and self-regulate. I still use it at times as a form of moving meditation. It helps me figure out problems, allows me to daydream, and clears my head."

Giwerc says that he was born physically and cognitively hyperactive—according to his mother, he kicked like crazy even in utero. As an infant and a young child, he went from climbing out of his crib, and later his bed, to being disruptive in school. "I was bored," states Giwerc, who would often find himself in the principal's office. "But I always had a smile on my face. I wasn't acting out because I was mad; I just needed the stimulation."

When the teacher lectured, if Giwerc was uninterested, he would become disruptive. "I tried any means of stimulation to get my brain going so that I could focus on the teacher's presentation," he says. "My hyperactive energy had no outlet. I'd get restless and squirm, unable to sit still in my chair. I'd blurt things out or shoot my hand into the air at inappropriate times or fidget conspicuously in my seat."

By the time he was six, Giwerc had been kicked out of two nursery schools and a kindergarten.

Things began to change when his third grade teacher, noticing his excess energy, arranged for him to join the other third grade class first thing in the morning because they went outside for 30 minutes of exercise as soon as the bell rang. It worked. He would then return to his own class better prepared to sit still.

"I was lucky," Giwerc says. "Throughout my school years, there was always one teacher or someone else who would stick their neck out for me."

Giwerc also credits sports, an area he excelled in, for saving his life. Basketball was his hands-down favorite, and playing on his junior high school team helped him cope with something that bothered him a great deal at the time—the fact that he wasn't placed in the accelerated academic program with all of his friends. "That made me feel lousy. But

I was on the basketball team—the only white guy there, in fact—and they weren't. So that helped my self-esteem."

Being in the mainstream academic program rather than the accelerated one also gave Giwerc the motivation to do well in school. "I always got good grades, and the teachers went out of their way for me because they saw an athlete who really cared about his education as well."

"Not that I didn't dwell on my failures, struggles, and challenges," Giwerc admits. "These recriminations plagued me throughout my childhood and young adulthood, until I was finally diagnosed and discovered that I wasn't inferior or broken after all."

Another lucky break for Giwerc came during his junior year of high school, when he was recruited by the basketball coach of an alternative high school program in his hometown of Albany, New York run by the teachers' college of State University of New York at Albany. "The school was small and taught by professors at the nearby university," Giwerc explains. "It was run like a college, and we didn't have to take the New York State Regents exams, which helped me as well."

He went on to Syracuse University and, in his freshman year, made the junior varsity basketball team as a walk-on. Yet as capable as he was on the court, Giwerc had difficulty learning the strategic plays. While his freshman coaches were patient, admiring his natural ball-handling and passing abilities, his learning impediment prevented him from making the team in his sophomore year.

Very disappointed but not deterred, Giwerc didn't give up. He made it through college, graduating with a Bachelors' Degree in Communications from Syracuse's prestigious S.I. Newhouse School of Public Communications. "I just knew I had to work a lot harder than anyone else," he says. "It was brutal for me to write a paper; what took others one hour probably took me five to ten. But I did it."

Giwerc credits his parents for his strength and perseverance. "They were Holocaust survivors, and even though my struggle was painful, it was nothing compared to what they had been through."

Shortly after graduation, Giwerc was living in Manhattan and working at his dream job as an advertising executive in sports marketing for the sales and promotion division of Young and Rubicam, one of the world's largest ad agencies. "It was an exciting time," he recalls. "I was 28 years old, single, making money, and working with nationally recognized clients and their brands. A recent graduate, and there I was managing important sports marketing relationships and promotional support across the country for well-known national brands of the giant Miller Brewing Company account."

As a sports enthusiast, Giwerc truly loved his job. Six sports field account executives, who were responsible for working with the NFL, NBA, and MLB teams in their particular regions, reported directly to him. He got rave reviews from his clients and the company's creative department, and while others spent hours preparing a pitch, he could invent a presentation on a dime and practice it in his head. He didn't need a script, just his mind-map—connected circles linking a few key-words together—that he would jot down on a napkin or an index card.

But as naturally as the creative side of his job came to him, Giwerc dreaded the administrative pressures of submitting expense accounts, writing reports, and sitting in one place long enough to process all the different things going on in his area of business. He intuitively knew that if he spent too much time in the administrative area of his profession, it was going to drain his energy and take him away from the areas of the business he was excelling in. So the paperwork piled up . . . until he reached out to his boss and asked for support.

"He was a great guy. He took me seriously and hired an administrative assistant who organized my files, took care of my expense reports, and eliminated the angst and frustration I felt." This also gave Giwerc a boost of confidence, making him realize that his company considered him important enough to provide him with the support he needed.

As time went on, however, despite his success and the support he received in the areas of his job that were difficult for him, Giwerc began to feel like something was missing.

"You would think that all of my professional accomplishments would have been enough to keep me satisfied and fulfilled," he says.

"However, after 12 years of working in a very high-pressure, albeit rewarding, profession, I started to wake up every day feeling empty."

Giwerc was 31 years old and had not yet been diagnosed with ADHD. After much mulling over the source of his discontent, he realized he was paying attention to a belief that was based on others' opinions of him. People perceived him as a very successful, confident, fun person in one of the most competitive professions and cities in the world—so he felt he had to keep going in that direction. But in reality, he was not paying attention to what his heart was seeking. He was searching for a sense of purpose, of meaning.

Fate stepped in when his agency offered him another promotion, on the condition that he move to Chicago. Still believing he should be heading down this career path, he accepted, and it was in Chicago that he met and married his wife Marla.

Marriage notwithstanding, Giwerc was still doing an incredible amount of traveling, and he was getting tired of being in a different city every other night. He was also given more campaign work which involved more strategic planning and more meetings, and he noticed that he was getting increasingly anxious. Despite all the travel, his day-to-day work essentially kept him chained to a desk, and the more sedentary he was, the harder things got.

His unease grew. "It got to the point where I wasn't being challenged anymore and I knew I needed to do something else, but I just didn't know what that something else was," Giwerc says. Eventually he decided to leave advertising and move back to Albany with his family to work with his father, a successful home builder for more than 30 years. Giwerc handled the marketing and sales for his dad's townhome and duplex apartment projects, but once again, despite his success, he began questioning whether or not this was the road for him. He admits that it was very difficult to work in the family business, especially with his own undiagnosed ADHD and his father's as-yet undiagnosed anxiety disorder and depression, all of which made their daily encounters very stressful.

It was now 1994, Giwerc was 38 years old, and everyone who knew anything at all about ADHD was telling him to read a book called *Driven to Distraction* by two Harvard psychiatrists with ADHD, Drs. John Ratey and Edward Hallowell (the latter of whom you've already met in Chapter 5). Giwerc acknowledges that a few of his close friends and family members knew how he had suffered many of the same problems these two doctors had—challenges related to interest, boredom, attention span, physical and cognitive hyperactivity, and more.

He vividly recalls the day he finally picked up *Driven to Distraction*. "When the book appeared before me one day in a bookstore window, I wandered in, pulled it off the shelf, and sat down to browse the pages. I didn't put it down until the bookstore closed."

That afternoon, Giwerc says, marked the start of his journey toward identifying his ADHD. Back then it wasn't easy, though, because most medical practitioners still believed that ADHD did not occur in adults. It was still thought to be something you simply grew out of when you reached adulthood. After a long search, however, Giwerc did find a doctor willing to diagnose his ADHD and prescribe medication to help him control it.

Still working for his dad, though, he was near the end of his rope. While the business was doing very well, it had become clear to him that this was not the kind of work he wanted to do. "I was thrilled to have moved on from advertising, but I knew I still hadn't found my true purpose," Giwerc says. "And that's when I came across an article in *Newsweek* about professional coaching."

Curious, he read through the article, and everything about this career seemed to speak to him. "The more I read about coaching, the more it resonated. I could feel in my heart that coaching was the right path for me." Giwerc signed up for a coaching teleclass and confirmed his gut reaction—he liked it. For a time he worked in the building business during the day, and at night took coaching classes and began to build a clientele. He chose to focus specifically on clients who, like him, had ADHD.

By 1998 he had exited the family business and had been coaching individual clients for a couple of years, finding happiness in the work. "Through this experience, I could see that there were so many people who needed support regarding their ADHD, and not enough coaches who understood their special challenges," Giwerc says. "I realized, too, that the organizations that were attempting to do this at the time were not aligned with my values and goals."

His deep desire to help as many people as possible with ADHD led Giwerc to his vision of creating a coaching school that would train coaches who wished to work specifically with ADHD clients. Giwerc's wife Marla became a trusted business partner; he relates that she was instrumental in helping him formulate his vision and make it a reality. Together, they founded the ADD Coaching Academy, where Giwerc serves as President and Marla holds the position of Director of Operations.

Today ADDCA is the largest and most successful ADHD coach training school in the world. Giwerc proudly states, "We have taught students from more than 21 countries and have eight instructors. In 2009, ADDCA became the only comprehensive ADHD coach training program accredited by the governing board of the coaching profession, the International Coach Federation (ICF)."

"This is what ignites my engine," says Giwerc, who has also served as President of ADDA from 2003 to 2006. "The part I love most is helping people. I really love to empower people, especially those who feel broken, by giving themselves permission to embrace their greatness—to go out and take action that will significantly improve the quality of their own lives and the lives of those who support them. I love acknowledging their strengths and reinforcing the evidence that these strengths exist within each one of them. So many people dwell on their weaknesses and the things they *don't* do well, rather than on their strengths and what they *do* do well."

Giwerc notes further, "I have realized that when I've been interested in something and kept moving, I always found success, but the opposite came up whenever something was difficult. Then my

ADHD showed up and the harder I tried, the more my brain shut down."

"The key to moving forward with your ADHD," he says, "is to find your strengths, and make sure those strengths are aligned with your passion. The vision you have for your life is just a vision until you put it into action. Realizing your purpose requires staying staunch in your commitment to it, no matter what doubts and fears may arise, and seeing where it takes you."

"What you want to do is create a life of passion, purpose, and possibility," Giwerc counsels. "Ask yourself the following four questions: What is it that I really, really want? What am I willing to do to get what I want? What's getting in the way? What's the story I am telling myself, and how must it change?"

Giwerc concludes with a look back on his life and career path thus far. "I have to do things that ignite my heart," he says. "I have been very fortunate to move from one profession to another and to learn from each one. I've now been coaching, training other coaches, and building and expanding a business based on a global vision for 16 or 17 years, and I still have no desire to do anything else. I have learned to trust my intuition, and that has served me well. I have to live this way; otherwise I would regret it. I have no regrets. I'm grateful for every moment."

Chapter 12

SOLDEN STANDS UP FOR WOMEN WITH ADHD

Life has been quite the journey for Sari Solden. Quiet and shy when young, unable to speak out in class or even among friends, she never dreamed that one day she would be the world-renowned author, presenter, and therapist that she is today.

"The tipping point for me came about when I was 40 and was diagnosed with learning disabilities and ADHD," Solden says. "The first day I took Ritalin, I told a story in front of a group of friends for five minutes and was in shock. What a relief to finally understand why I had struggled in so many ways!"

Solden says she quickly began to make up for lost time, discovering that all those years weren't really wasted, just waiting to be unleashed. "That diagnosis and subsequent therapy had a pretty immediate impact and made it possible for me to move forward," she remembers.

Growing up in Detroit, Michigan, Solden says she did fine in the right classes with the right teachers. Looking back, now she can see she was already beginning to compensate for her ADHD by turning almost every assignment she could into a drama or quiz show. She would fall back on her creativity because trying to put together anything linear was just too difficult.

Solden says she was really thrown for a loop when she entered seventh grade and was placed in honors classes. Despite the fact that she was smart, she found she couldn't keep up, and the teachers were very demanding. In addition to her undiagnosed ADHD, Solden's handwriting was very poor, and on all her papers the teachers would write things like, "very messy, see me" or "a second-grader could have written this."

As a result, Solden began to develop psychosomatic symptoms in order to avoid going to school. She would tell her parents she had a stomachache or the flu. She also became very anxious and felt bad about herself because she couldn't seem to do what the other girls could, such as figuring out how to dress appropriately.

"Life was confusing," Solden says. "There was always such a split in my life between the things that were very hard for me to do versus very easy."

She remembers how she always seemed to collect a lot of papers and how her locker and desk were a mess. She says she wouldn't participate in most classes, deathly afraid of being wrong. In classes where sensitivity and creativity were valued, however, she was successful.

College presented even more challenges. "Living independently requires you to rely even more on your executive functioning skills," says Solden, who now recognizes how compromised those skills are for those with ADHD.

Time management, priority-setting, organization, and decision-making were all areas where she had found support when living at home. Once she was on her own, she recalls, "I couldn't figure out how to cook, my room was a mess—all those things that had been done for me, now I had to figure out how to do myself. I didn't know what had hit me."

Academically Solden did well in college, although she admits she had an odd way of studying. "The only way I could learn the material was to rewrite every word of the textbook over and over and over." It was also difficult for her to find a place to study where she wouldn't be distracted.

"I was always moving around a lot, trying to find places where I wouldn't be disturbed," Solden says. "I was lonely, felt disconnected, and was more focused on just trying to keep up. I loved school and learning, but it seemed like I was having a much harder time than others."

Shortly after graduating from the University of Michigan, Solden married, moved to Florida, and tried "the whole housewife thing," she says, only to discover that lifestyle wasn't going to work for her. "I thought I wanted to conform, but in a way, ADHD saved me from that type of life."

Like many women with ADHD, she found that raising a child and taking care of a home were tasks that certainly did not utilize her strengths. "Grocery shopping, laundry, cooking and cleaning—it was all overwhelming and difficult," she says.

As a result, Solden experienced a lot of guilt because society tells us that this is what women should be able to do. Her book *Women with Attention Deficit Disorder* poignantly depicts how, in addition to the guilt, women such as herself experience deep shame as they find themselves unable to live up to expectations ingrained early in life.

After five years in Florida, Solden relocated to the West Coast and spent the next 20 years in the California Bay Area, where she wrote a great deal of creative non-fiction. This included pieces describing the work she had done with patients in mental hospitals, as a social service worker with people on public assistance, and in farm labor camps in Florida.

"Every time things got too disorganized, I would move. I was a pioneer; I was looking for new horizons where individuality was valued more than it was when I grew up," Solden says.

In 2005 she remarried and, with her second husband, opened a rock-and-roll music school in Marin County, CA where kids, teens, and adults were placed in their own rock bands depending on their musical ability. "It was great for them musically and for their self-esteem," says

Solden, who played drums in one of the adult bands. "Many of these children had ADHD, some were from low-income families, and others were just students of all ages gaining the self-confidence that comes from learning to work together in this way."

Solden and her husband also produced children's videos with positive messages. Previously Solden had developed her own programs for several years using the creative arts, including dance, music, and writing, as emotional and therapeutic vehicles for children both with and without special needs.

After a while, however, Solden realized that she needed to get back to what she had initially set out to do, and returned to school to pursue her original goal of becoming a psychotherapist. She began to work on her Master's Degree in Clinical Counseling with an emphasis on cross-cultural counseling, and earned a license in marriage and family therapy. Solden went on to serve as the specialist on adult ADHD for the Family Service Agency of Marin County.

While serving as an intern there, Solden began to interface with the office that handled special programs for minorities with mental health issues and learning disabilities, and they suggested she take the same battery of tests her clients had to undergo in order to understand their experience. When she did, she received quite a surprise when the results showed the "wild differential in her abilities."

Armed with this new information, Solden consulted a neuropsychologist, took more tests, and was told she had ADHD and learning disabilities. She says the tests confirmed for her that she was, in fact, extremely bright, but that her struggles over the years had been due to an armload of learning challenges. This realization made her feel much better about herself. "The diagnosis was a relief, as well as very validating."

The combination of medication and therapy was what made it possible for her to be successful, Solden says. Ritalin, in particular, gave her a new lease on life. "All of a sudden I began to speak up at agency group meetings. I could actually go shopping without being overwhelmed or distracted by the piped-in music," she says.

Solden began writing and speaking more, and after some real soul-searching, decided that working in an agency was not a good fit for her. She eventually moved back to Michigan, where she opened up a private practice as a psychotherapist working with adults with ADHD and their partners.

Solden wrote her first book, *Women with Attention Deficit Disorder*, in 1995. It has now sold well over 150,000 copies worldwide and has been translated into German, Japanese, and Danish. Her second book, *Journeys Through ADDulthood*, grew out of 12 years of working with men and women with ADHD, during which time she developed a framework for understanding the difference between those who get stuck following their diagnosis and those who are able to grow and move on.

Solden also became a prominent speaker at both national and international ADHD conferences, and has served on the professional advisory board of ADDA as well as on the program conference committee for CHADD.

"Conferences are not just places to gain information, but to connect with people who have the same kind of perspective as you do," she says. "When you're around those who struggle with similar challenges, you realize how much you are hiding on a day-to-day basis, and you can let go. It's seeing people in their own culture, being with your own tribe. It's very empowering."

Today, Solden both hosts and presents on www.ADDJourneys.com, her online community for adults with ADHD.

She emphasizes the importance of acceptance, of not hating yourself for who you are. "It's seeing yourself as whole—that includes your strengths and weaknesses. It's learning to live with much more chaos than other people live with, but continuing to move forward."

Solden urges those who think they have to wait to get better before moving toward their vision to instead use their personal struggles and adversity as motivation to keep going. "I've been healed over and over again by writing and speaking, and hearing about other people's experiences," she says. "It's a long journey, but it's about achieving greater self-awareness and fulfillment."

Chapter 13

LINDA LAMBDIN HAS HER OWN BEAT—ROCK ON!

Linda Lambdin marches to the beat of her own drummer and wouldn't have it any other way. In her own words, she's a dreamer and a visionary. "I'm very intuitive. My way of seeing and acting in the world has a deep and positive effect on many people," she says.

Lambdin believes these strengths are a direct result of her ADHD. "Although my ADD does hamper me when it comes to paperwork and certain other tasks, I don't see it as a deficit, but as a gift."

Lambdin was not diagnosed with ADHD until the age of 50. "It's been fascinating to have a better understanding of what makes my brain tick," the K-8 charter school principal says enthusiastically.

"As a small child I was always really well liked, but a dreamy little thing," she relates. "I did well in school and the other kids loved me, but all the teachers would write on my report card, 'Linda is not living up to her potential.'"

As time went on, however, Lambdin was always given the leadership roles. She was head of the safety squad in elementary school, Girl Scout troop president, captain of the field hockey, gymnastics, and lacrosse teams, and a cheerleader. "I always succeeded," she says, but admits that her two best friends helped her every inch of the way.

"They were my support team, Suzy and Missy. One later became a doctor and the other a lawyer. I was an A student, but it was because my friends would keep me on track. They would remind me when writing assignments were due, or when I had to study for an upcoming test. Sometimes they would even act out what I needed to know since I had a difficult time studying."

Lambdin, still not aware of her ADHD in college, says she made a good intuitive choice in designing her own major, one which concentrated on education and society and how they influence each other. "Looking back, I can now see what a good decision that was, because I couldn't focus on anything I wasn't interested in."

Lambdin returned to Denmark, where she had previously been a high school exchange student during her sophomore year of college. She spent this year observing many innovative alternative schools. She also attended one of their "folk schools" (similar to our community colleges) to continue her research for her major.

Lambdin was greatly influenced by her experience in Denmark, which is rated one of the happiest countries in the world. "The people vote for higher taxes," she says. "Homelessness is not a problem, and the country provides medical care from cradle to grave. Free education is also accessible to anyone who wants it for as long as they want it. It is this idea of creating human beings who have compassion for one another, and take care of one another, that caught my attention."

This positive experience followed Lambdin home. "Upon my return, my advisor, who just happened to be the Dean of Education, must have recognized something in me, because she told me she would waive all education requirements but still allow me to graduate with a degree in education. She said if I tried to attend the required education classes it would ruin me, and she was right," Lambdin states. "I never would have made it through those classes. I wouldn't have done the work, because I intuitively knew that much of what they were teaching ran counter to how people really learn and grow into whole, self-actualized beings."

Her advisor felt those classes would have stifled her creativity. Instead, she gave Lambdin books to read, and met with her frequently to discuss her developing educational beliefs.

Lambdin's first teaching job was in a one-room schoolhouse in southern Maine called The School Around Us. There were only 30 students, encompassing children from kindergarten through the eighth grade, and it was a fully democratic, parent-run cooperative. "The parents talked about educational philosophy and looked at the factors that create innovative, whole, intelligent human beings who grow up to be leaders, not followers," Lambdin explains. "The school emphasized involvement in the local and global community, social and environmental awareness, and kindness of heart."

"At the time I was living in a converted chicken coop on a farm and leading a very unconventional alternative lifestyle," she recalls. "We had an outhouse, and in the winter we had to take a toboggan to get water from a well. It was like living in *Little House on the Prairie*."

Lambdin taught at The School Around Us for six years, then left to travel across the United States, up through Canada and Alaska. "I knew that I would probably be a teacher for life, so I needed to broaden my sense of the world," she says. "If not, all you end up doing is teaching your students how to exist in school, not how to exist in life."

Joel, a boyfriend who much later became Lambdin's husband, taught her how to hop freight trains. "We camped all over," she says, "and in between we would work odd jobs to earn just enough money to return to hitchhiking." Lambdin's resume includes stints as a beekeeper, cocktail waitress, and shrimp and crab factory worker. She can also boast of being a deckhand on a crab fishing boat, a cook on a whale-watching ship, and a parquet floor layer. "My résumé should also say that I was terrible at each of these jobs," Lambdin adds. "The dreaminess of the ADD brain was certainly not an asset to me in these capacities."

Lambdin admits that her mother was very worried about her, "but for me these unusual experiences were magical. They fit with my dream world. I always wanted something bigger than this life, than the narrow corridor that most people walk through. I always had a bigger vision."

That bigger vision included one very cold winter when Lambdin agreed to be the caretaker of an uninhabited island off the coast of British Columbia which was rumored to house a ghost town. "Having unlimited time to live in my dream world was very compelling to me," she says, talking about why she chose to take on this particular job. "Dream time for me was so important to me then—and still is to this day. I spend a lot of time lying on my bed halfway in this world and halfway out of this world. Some of my best ideas come to me then. Of course a lot of them never come to fruition, but the ones that are supposed to, do."

It was during that long, cold winter that Lambdin admits she began thinking a lot about sunny California, and once off the island she headed there. The northern coastal city of Santa Cruz became her home, and shortly after her arrival Lambdin read a book called *Joy in the Classroom* that totally changed her life. The book's author, Stephanie Herzog, lived just 20 minutes away from Lambdin, and was the head of Evergreen, another K-8 school with under 100 students. Lambdin contacted her, was hired on the spot, and worked there until the school folded two years later.

At Evergreen the students were taught meditation, telepathy, energy awareness, and conflict resolution, in addition to the usual reading, writing, arithmetic, social studies and science. The children would start their day with meditation and then choose between creative writing and art before moving on to their other subjects. Then once a week they would learn a "chakra," or energy center in the body, through movement and theater.

When Evergreen shut its doors Lambdin was hired by the Santa Cruz city school system, where she worked for the next 14 years trying to figure out how to make it work in a more traditional classroom of 30 students. "I was always aware of a little voice inside of me, telling me that I was here to try to change the face of public education, to make my contribution," she says.

And she eventually got her chance. Today Lambdin is the principal of a small charter school which she agreed to run "as long as I can be the visionary. When they need someone to be more of a traditional administrator, then it's time for me to leave. As a principal I don't administrate in the same way that any other administrator does," she confesses. "I'm gifted by being attuned to other forms of communication and energy levels."

Lambdin admits, however, that she still has difficulty with details and paperwork. Having the right support around her is essential. "I have other people do all the pieces that I can't do, so that I can do the pieces I do well," she says. "For example, everyone at my school knows not to give me any important documents. They show them to me then file them in their own files. When I am working on a project, I always have others hold onto the paper work and all of the supporting materials in between sessions. I can lose a piece of paper faster than you can blink."

Since being diagnosed with ADHD, Lambdin has, however, learned how to keep it simple. She has very little clutter in her home and, as a result of her own issues with organization, has trained teachers to check up on their students' backpacks. "Kids who have what I have cannot keep track of everything," Lambdin states. "So all they need is one spiral notebook with self-contained pages that can't fall out."

Organizational skills are important, she says, especially for those with ADHD. "The key is finding a method that works for you. I have one hardbound notebook that I write everything in, and a fanny pack that holds my calendar, keys, and iPhone. Should I stray from my system, invariably something gets lost." Lambdin also keeps a huge whiteboard next to her bedroom mirror where she writes everything down that she needs to remember to bring with her the next day. She pays her bills online, and to stay in touch with friends, she never leaves a date without scheduling the next one. "Otherwise it's shocking how easy it is to forget."

Lambdin admits that parenting her son was difficult as a result of her ADHD. "I thought that being a teacher would prepare me for being a mom, but that wasn't the case. At the time, I didn't understand why. In retrospect, my ADHD diagnosis explains a lot. It was so much easier for me to focus on 30 children in a classroom than to keep my focus on just one child. I was always berating myself for losing attention, and it was challenging for me to keep up with the housework, laundry, grocery shopping, and other domestic responsibilities. That wasn't the vision that I'd had for myself as a parent."

Lambdin now looks back and realizes that she should have been content with what she *could* give her son as a parent, and been glad there were people close by to fill in the gaps. Helping Lambdin reach this point of acceptance in her life is Joel Slattengren, her husband of eleven years. "He's the one I hopped freight trains with years ago," Lambdin says. "He always kept in touch, and I finally realized that I shouldn't marry someone as a way to please my parents, but because I'd found someone who is right for me."

Lambdin glows when talking about her husband's love and support. "Joel, who also has ADHD, reminds me every day how much he loves me and how lovable I am. He has so much faith in me, and knowing that really helps with my self-esteem."

Another big step for Lambdin was throwing out 30 journals filled with self-improvement lists and what she refers to as "whining about myself." Today she records only positive thoughts in her journal. "Even if I have had a horrible day, I write whatever good things did happen, and then draw something at the top of the page to make it look beautiful," she says. "So the day looks beautiful on paper, and it shifts my thinking. I love my journals and I love my life."

Chapter 14

BEST FATHERS IN THE WORLD

Hands down, dads with ADHD might just win the "Best Father in the World" award when it comes to having fun.

"I'm like a grown-up kid and they love it," says Joe Elfassy, who has learned how to be a clown, a juggler, and an amateur chef. "My girls have a dad who can do things most other dads can't."

"I'm not afraid to try anything," says this stay-at-home dad. "I'm all about spontaneity. We garden, we build things, I teach them how to repair things. I'm very hands-on, and whatever I do I involve them in it," he says of his six- and ten-year-old daughters.

"The kids know that if they want to have a good time, go see Dad," Elfassy continues. No matter what they want to try, I'm in. No matter how difficult or unrealistic their requests, I will try to figure out a way that we can do it. And I am always able to see the funny side of any given situation."

Duane Gordon, also father to two daughters—one of whom has ADHD herself—echoes the same sentiments. He laughingly remembers when his youngest daughter was in the first grade and needed to dress up as a train engine for a Christmas pageant. "Between the two of us, we went kind of crazy . . . okay, it was mostly me," he admits. "By the time we had finished, there was even smoke coming out of the engine.

The only problem was once she put it on she couldn't lift it, and we had to dismantle a good portion of it."

On a roll, Gordon recalls more holiday memories. "Another Christmas my daughter Kyrie and I took it upon ourselves to put the lights up outside to decorate the house for Christmas. "We figured we could do it up right, and by the time we were finished, planes were probably going off track because our house was so bright with all the lights covering our house."

He recalls with fondness, "These are memories that my daughters still have today—of all the crazy things they did with Dad. Most definitely one of the plus sides of being a father with ADHD is coming up with so many wacky ideas and doing strange stuff without bothering to think whether or not it makes sense or it's logical. I just go for it."

Even now, although Gordon's daughters are in their 20s, they come to him to problem-solve or brainstorm. He says that they can always rely on him for ideas. Last year when his oldest daughter, now 28, was working on her Ph.D. in psychology, she would turn to Gordon for ideas for research topics and he was always able to help. "I can think of great questions or ideas even if I don't totally understand the subject matter," he states.

(Today, Gordon's daughter is a psychologist doing research at the University of North Carolina at Chapel Hill. She is a post-doctoral fellow, wife and mother of a nine-month-old little boy.)

"One of the traits that makes ADHD dads the best dads in the world is our curiosity and willingness to learn about the things our kids are interested in," said Jay Carter. "ADHD dads can hyperfocus with their children on whatever the latest and greatest thing piquing their interest is. Then when the child's attention wanes from that particular area of fascination, so does the dad's, where other dads might become frustrated they invested so much time and energy now that their kid has lost interest," Carter points out.

However, it's not all fun and games for these dads, as they struggle in the same ways that anyone else with ADHD does. Joe Pecile, father of two boys in their early 20s, believes that a father with ADHD can be more understanding as opposed to judgmental because of his own challenges. Since Pecile's ADHD diagnosis he has learned the importance of feeling whole and not flawed because of his challenges and, as a result, wants to teach his own children those very same lessons. Having dealt with feelings of failure and self-doubt, this dad urges other parents to do all they can to build self-confidence in their children, starting with acknowledging their successes and emphasizing their strengths over their weaknesses.

Elfassy agrees, although he realizes that when he is off his medication he can forget how young his children are and expect a bit too much from them. "When off my meds, I can begin to feel like everything they do is against me," he says. "With medication, I remember that they are just kids." Admitting that inconsistency with his medications is a challenge he faces as a father with ADHD, Elfassy acknowledges that when he hasn't taken them he tends to react to the smallest stimuli even though it is really not that big a deal. He says his children notice the difference, so when he's forgotten to take his medication even his youngest will say, "Daddy, you've gone crazy, take your meds."

Gordon also agrees that during his daughter's teen years, it was difficult not to overreact. "When a kid does something, you react immediately without thinking of the consequences and whether or not the situation is really that important. The same impulsivity that makes me ready for anything fun often leads me to say things I regret later."

Pecile has had similar problems, but he points out that once he learned about his ADHD, his family relationships improved. The understanding helps him retreat to a neutral corner of the ring rather than engaging immediately in a more negative way.

Carter, too, experiences impulsivity, but believes that sometimes it can be positive because it helps him to reward his children's behavior quickly. "The trick is to make sure that our impulsive reaction has the appropriate amount of correction or reinforcement," he says.

"One of the biggest challenges of being a father with ADHD is trying to create consistency in the way that we work with our children,"

Carter says. "Most kids, especially kids with ADHD, do well with structure: going to bed at the same time, getting up at about the same time, having the same expectations for homework and chores around the house. But for dads with ADHD, this can really be challenging. We strive for some level of consistency in our own lives, and even that's hard to do sometimes."

He elaborates: "Dads with ADHD struggle with social cues in social situations, but we also struggle with the social cues around our own family. We can sometimes have difficulty in picking up on some of the things a child is going through, and may not be quite as able to step in with the appropriate response."

Forgetfulness is another challenge of fathers with ADHD, Elfassy says. On a recent Saturday, his wife suggested he take his daughters to a local fair while she was at work. He planned to do just that, but woke up thinking what a perfect day it was to build a garden, and got so involved working with his kids in the backyard that he totally forgot about the fair. Elfassy felt bad that he let his daughters down. He knows they were disappointed, and when things like that happen, he feels that he's let himself down as well.

Too much activity can be another challenge, says Carter. "As dads with ADHD, we're often very busy because there are so many things we like to do and we don't always make time or set aside time to be there for our kids."

Pecile shares another problem he experiences. "One of the challenges of being a father with ADHD is making sure that my game is up to par. ADHD often impairs one's ability to be on top of one's game, and that provides additional challenges as a parent with it."

He is thankful his diagnosis was uncovered before more time slipped by. "I like to say I got my ADHD from them," he jokes of his children, acknowledging his gratitude that their condition helped uncover his own. "After my diagnosis, my self-perception and my perception of my sons changed for the better." Pecile says it helped him to learn how ADHD affects the pre-frontal cortex of the brain and the areas that involve impulsivity, focus, time management, and problem-solving.

"This diagnosis was a long-awaited explanation as to why I was so different from many of my counterparts," he says. "The knowledge I gained about ADHD and how it has impacted me has helped me become a better father. It is often said, 'Know thyself,' and I would like to think that teaching that to my boys is one of the most important lessons I can pass on to them."

Gordon offers this to other ADHD dads: "My advice would be to remember that life will happen anyway. You don't have to push it; you don't have to force it. There is very little you are upset about today that is a matter of life or death. When we are going through a particular situation, it seems like the end of the world—that it's 'do or die'—but it's really not. Lighten up; don't take everything so seriously. I'd add that it would be a good idea to be as quick with an apology when we hurt someone's feelings as we are to jump into an adventure."

Carter agrees. "The most important thing is to help your children know they are loved. That is the single biggest and most important thing they need. Try to give affirmation as often as possible. Tell them how much you appreciate the things they do well, and not just with empty compliments like, 'I like your blue shirt.' Tell them you appreciate some of the things they do or some of the character traits that they have."

For fathers with ADHD who are struggling from a parenting standpoint—whether it's consistency with things around the house or emotional issues—Carter advises getting help. He says that if you're feeling challenged helping your kids with homework on a regular basis, staying organized, or just dealing with things related to your own ADHD, then it might be time to seek out a coach or get some help from a family member or friend in dealing with those issues.

Elfassy's advice to other ADHD fathers is built around acceptance of one's diagnosis. "It's just another facet of life. We all have something. I have ADHD, but it's just a part of who I am."

He closes with this thought: "At the end of the day, your life is just a story and everything that happens to you is just a part of that story. You might as well make it a positive one. There's always somebody who has something worse than you, so just be grateful and go with it."

Here are some tips by Duane Gordon for fathers dealing with both their families and their own ADHD:

- Don't stick your head in the sand. If you have ADHD, your family is affected. Face it and deal with it. Ignorance is *not* bliss, and denial is selfish. Your entire family wants you to succeed. They are willing, even eager, to help. Just ask.

- Routines rule. Most people struggle to be creative and spontaneous but it's your natural state. Chaos reigns, but not much gets done. Develop routines, systems, and habits to provide structure and improve productivity for the entire family.

- Work with your strengths. Divide household chores according to each person's aptitudes, not with stereotypical divisions of labor. If you're a morning person, help the kids get ready for school. If home renovations aren't your thing, outsource them—or let your wife handle them!

- Don't "share" chores. Give each person, children included, full responsibility (and sufficient authority) for any given chore. Asking for non-specific "help around the house" rarely gives the desired results.

- Your child's ADHD is not your ADHD. ADHD-friendly approaches that work for you might not work for your child. Give them responsibility, but allow them to figure out how to do things their way.

- <u>Anger is a habit</u>. If you struggle to control your emotions, don't dismiss it as, "That's just the way I am." Angry outbursts never improve family life. It will be challenging, but you can change even that habit.

- <u>Laugh</u>. Never take yourself too seriously. Teach your children to laugh, and laugh along with them. Your ADHD will provide plenty of opportunities! And isn't that the best legacy to leave your children?

- <u>Fake it until you make it</u>. Success is a journey. Set a cheerful tone in your home, regardless of your mood. Feel bad? Smile. And if you don't feel like smiling, all the more reason to slap one on anyway.

- <u>Accept</u>. Love is not real love unless it's unconditional. Acceptance is the best gift you can give your children. Accept them regardless of what they are, and regardless of what they are not. Then give yourself the same gift.

Chapter 15

THIS ATTENTION COACH HAS
WALKED IN YOUR SHOES

"**M**uch of the success that I have had in my life has been the result of my giving up what I was 'supposed to do' and figuring out how to do things the way my brain works," says Jeff Copper of DIG Coaching and Attention Talk Radio.

Copper, diagnosed with dyslexia and learning disabilities at a young age, grew up struggling with many of the same issues that those with ADHD must deal with. In fifth grade his reading and math scores were comparable to those of a second- or third-grader despite his mother's best efforts to help him succeed.

Copper says his mom, who was a teacher, would often wake him up at 4:30 a.m. to help him catch up on the schoolwork he hadn't been able to finish the night before. He also worked with a slew of tutors over the years, "but they just grew frustrated with me."

Because of his learning disabilities, in order for Copper to learn something he must understand the 'why' of it. "I need to understand how things are in relationship with each other," he explains.

As an attention coach, Copper says he has the unique advantage of having "walked in the shoes of those whose brains are wired differently." Like people with ADHD and other attention problems," he says, "I, too, was frustrated, stuck, and overwhelmed."

He explains: "Metaphorically, having different brain wiring is like being born left-handed in a right-handed world. Society and the self-help sections in bookstores are quick to suggest right-handed solutions."

Extending the metaphor, ADHD coaches help those with ADHD attend to the fact that they were born left-handed. When they do so, Copper says, then solutions that fit their unique brain wiring become more obvious.

"If we were all the same, there wouldn't be such a thing as left-handed golf clubs. The fact is, we are all different. ADHD coaches help those with ADHD find ADHD solutions."

Copper says he loves helping his clients learn how to refocus, paying attention to their strengths rather than their weaknesses. He knows that if it wasn't for his own natural ability and passion for swimming, for instance, he might not be where he is today. The sport helped raise his self-esteem, an issue Copper struggled with because of his lackluster performance in school. Copper says that despite the daily hour-long drive to and from swim practice, his parents supported him because swimming was something he was good at.

Copper continued to swim in high school, describing an even more grueling schedule that began with a 4:00 a.m. wake-up call, an hour's drive to practice, two hours of swimming, an hour's drive to school, and a full day of classes, followed by another two-hour swim practice in the afternoon. "I wouldn't get home until 7:30 p.m., with little time left in the day to eat, pack up for the next day, and do homework," he says.

By his junior year in high school, however, Copper was a top-ranked competitive swimmer and made the USA Swimming National Championships. He participated in the Olympic Team Trials in 1980 and again in 1984. Swimming was also Copper's ticket into college. He says he knew full well that he would never get in based on his poor SAT scores.

"I was motivated to keep swimming because I was good at it, and despite my academic struggles, I had dreams of going to college one day," says Copper, who went to Indiana University on a swimming scholarship. "But when I got to school, I was there by myself. I had no one to fall back on, and within ten days I'll never forget, I was calling home and telling my parents I couldn't keep up and didn't know what I was going to do."

Copper was determined, though. He realized that if he was going to graduate, he had to figure out how his brain worked. Slowly but surely, he let go of the feeling that he had to read every word of the assigned texts and began to focus on the first line of each paragraph, paying attention to the gist of what was being said. He never missed class, took many notes, and asked a lot of questions.

Writing research papers, however, presented another hurdle for Copper to get over. Just the idea of writing a paper was overwhelming, he admits. But once again, he learned to step back and look at how his brain worked best. In one of those "a-ha" moments, he realized that if he could interview an expert in the field that he had to write about, he could write the paper using the interviewee's quotes. It worked, and he remembers getting an A— on his first research paper.

"All of a sudden my grades went back up, and I figured okay, I'm smart, I can do this," Copper recalls. "But then I made the mistake of loading up on classes my sophomore year, and the wheels came off."

Once again Copper regrouped. He concentrated on what he should be paying attention to so that he could narrow the scope of what he was studying at any given moment and focus on it tightly.

Copper's hard work paid off, and in 1985 he graduated with a Bachelor's Degree in Public Affairs. Soon after, he was selling group insurance and pension plans for Aetna, later switching companies to Northwestern National and moving to Florida, where he also began participating in triathlons. "I was pretty good at it, and several of the people I trained with went pro."

Things had finally seemed to settle into place for Copper. "I was an athlete, a sales guy, and really successful for four or five years making more money than I'd ever dreamed of," he says. As time went on, he married, started a family, and began to turn his competitive edge from athletics to business, even returning to school to get his MBA. Copper says he found school a lot easier that time around, as he was able to apply what he had already been practicing in the business world. He went from a 2.8 grade point average as an undergraduate to a 3.8 in graduate school.

In the years that followed, his wife was promoted in her career to the point where they were both traveling weekly, and the nanny was spending more nights with their children than they were. At this point Copper decided to step away from the business world and stay home to play "Mr. Mom." It was during this time that Copper's wife's company hired an executive coach to assist her, and this is how the idea of coaching as a career change option presented itself to him. Copper says his wife thought it just might be a good fit for him, and he recalls how a psychologist friend also pointed out how organized he was, telling him that he would make a good coach for those with ADHD.

Soon Copper embraced the idea, and he can now boast of being a graduate of the Coaches Training Institute (CTI) certification program, the ADD Coach Academy (ADDCA), and the ADDCA Entrepreneur Class of May 2007. "Coaching comes easily for me," he says. "I got though life paying attention to what was being attended to, which is the key in coaching attention in others."

Next, someone turned Copper onto BlogTalkRadio.com, and he soon started his own audio blog, which eventually morphed into Attention Talk Radio, a narrowcast Internet-based radio show that airs at 8:00 p.m. Eastern Standard time every Wednesday night.

In 2008 Copper attended the CHADD conference in Cleveland, Ohio and began approaching some of the presenters there, asking them if they would appear on his radio show. "Everyone I asked said yes, and at the next year's conference, I got even more people to talk." Since then Copper has also started Attention Talk Video and Attention Talk News, and is currently in the process of bringing all of his endeavors under one umbrella.

"As a result of what I do, I bring a unique perspective to my coaching," Copper says. "The education I have received from interviewing and getting to know so many of the experts in the field of ADHD is invaluable."

"ADHD is not an attention issue," he emphasizes, "but an issue of self-regulation. You have to learn how to pay attention to the right things. Don't try harder—try different."

Chapter 16

LEARN SELF-COMPASSION

Barbara Luther's struggle with her weight began on the Missouri farm where she grew up, and where her mother baked a double batch of chocolate chip cookies and two cakes every day. "We were a big farm family," Luther says. "We worked hard and ate robustly."

In high school her father began to call her fat. Despite that, she didn't notice the pounds pile on while in college. "I wasn't really paying attention to it," Luther says. "I'm one of those ADDers who lives in my head, not paying much attention to my body."

In fact, back then Luther didn't even know that many of her struggles, weight-related and otherwise, were due to ADHD, as she was not diagnosed with it until the age of 45. Luther was also not aware, until recently, of the link between ADHD, obesity, and eating disorders. "More than 60 percent of those seeking medical weight loss help also have ADHD," said Luther, who became an ADHD coach in 1997. "The medical field is just beginning to understand this link."

According to some recent studies, Luther explains, there is a possible link between ADHD and the gene known to be associated with drug addiction and impulsivity. These studies show a possible connection between ADHD symptoms and obese adults who binge on food.

If this connection pans out, weight loss treatments would need to be different for those with ADHD vs. those without it.

"You can know quite a bit and still not really understand how your ADHD is impacting you," Luther says. "We may have thought we understood it, but we didn't grasp the strong connection between the difficulty around impulsivity and problems with weight loss. Yet when you think about it, proper weight management relies on the ability to control your response to temptation. Lack of self-regulation, poor decision-making, sleep issues, and depression—all these can adversely affect someone trying to lose weight.

"And eating is self-soothing," adds Luther. "When the brain is tired or stressed, we don't know what to do to give it support. So we often get up and grab something to eat. We fall into a mindless unhealthy habit." She goes on to explain that this is why there's also a strong correlation between ADHD and alcoholism or drug addiction. We impulsively try something new, such as taking a drug, drinking a bit too much or binge eating. We do this new thing a few times because it is novel or fulfills a need, and we discover that it feels good. Then we become caught in the addictive habit loop.

"Plus, the temptations are so numerous when it comes to food," Luther points out emphatically. "You can't drive a mile without seeing fast food signs, and for those of us with ADHD, self-regulation is very difficult. We may be able to ignore the first few signs, but by the time we see the tenth one, we pull in."

According to Luther, mindfulness plays a huge role in managing the impulse to binge. "At least it does for me," she says. "On my own personal journey, I had to address mindfulness first. I had to stop and look at what I was eating every day. I wrote down everything that went into my mouth and made sure I weighed myself every day."

That kind of structure is essential, she insists. "It helped me learn what my signals were. I got into the habit of asking myself, 'Is that a hunger signal, or an emotional one?' Writing it all down helped me remember."

Luther, who lost 80 pounds before getting married at age 21, understands people's reluctance to do this. She has yo-yoed up and down several times since then, always regaining the weight she'd lost and then some.

"We resist the practice of recording our eating big time," she says. However, she stresses that while we feel it's a hassle, it's important that we do it anyway. "Personally, when I get away from writing down what I eat, thinking, 'I know how to eat now,' the weight comes back on," Luther confesses. "If I'm not writing it down, I can't remember what I've eaten throughout the day, and then I'm off eating too much again," Luther says.

"Dieting takes so much focus on something that just doesn't seem that important to us ADDers," she continues, pointing out how often those with ADHD find themselves ravenous but with nothing to eat in the house. "Food prep and menu planning is boring, and it's no fun to figure out what to purchase if you even manage to get yourself to the grocery store."

What did help Luther was learning how to keep certain things in the house for quick meals that she could throw together without a lot of hassle. "I had my five favorite breakfasts, lunches, and dinners and could turn to those in a pinch," she says.

About four years ago, when she had once again lost a considerable amount of weight (over 100 pounds), Luther decided she was tired of feeling awful. At first she simply started eating a Mediterranean-type diet and recording what she ate. "I wanted to ease my way into changing my eating habits," Luther explains. "I didn't want to diet; I wanted to find a plan that I could live with and lose the weight slowly. I never set a bigger goal than ten pounds at a time."

But she became curious. "After losing the first ten pounds, then the second, I just started feeling better and wanted to see if I could feel even better than that."

As she began to lose more weight, she started feeling very good indeed. "I was proud of myself," Luther says, "and I was enjoying my body for the first time since I was a teenager. My knees didn't hurt. My back didn't hurt." Once she'd dropped 50 pounds, Luther even started working out.

"And I didn't feel deprived," she stresses. "That's so important when it comes to weight loss. For every human being, every mammal that feels confined, restricted, or controlled—we're going to lash out. That's what diets do to us. And if you start feeling deprived and don't address that, you're going to self-destruct." Even when successfully losing weight, Luther says she would allow herself a tiny bit of dark chocolate every day, which went a long way toward keeping that deprived feeling at bay. Whenever her eating is under control, she explains, she can even go out with friends, eat and drink freely, and then go back to her healthier way of eating the next day.

Unfortunately that has proven more difficult for her in recent years, partly due to depression and some hormone fluctuations that hit her about two or three years ago. "I just couldn't sustain things as well," she says. "I lost it through the holidays. The depression just dragged me down." She reached out for help, but nothing worked. "I couldn't even get the doctors to hear me. I was scared of my own impulsivity and needed additional support."

Luther turned to David Giwerc, a friend and colleague and the founder of ADDCA. Giwerc helped her understand that when something is out of harmony, we need to pay attention to that disharmony and the signals that manifest in our bodies in response. He reminded her that inattentive types need to work that much harder to observe those patterns. "t is all about the power of the pause, he told me, which I already knew, but was not practicing," Luther says. "It is so important to learn how to identify the signals that are being sent to your brain before they expand into a dangerous situation that can compromise your physical and/or mental health."

Giwerc helped her truly believe that depression can create a barrier to the successful patterns already established in our brains, which is what was happening to Luther. Even though she had experienced success before, having learned how to pause and consciously make the right choices and decisions that created consistent and positive results, the depression took her right back to her old days. "'But if you were successful once before, you can do it again,' he told me," Luther says. "He reminded me that positive psychology is about savoring the success and taking those learning experiences into the next phase. It is the savoring and reappraisal that makes resilient people come back and take action in new and improved ways."

Luther already had all this knowledge, but it hadn't been anchored as a "knowing," a new belief. In retrospect, Luther thinks that perhaps she had to regain some of the weight to learn further lessons, particularly around negative self-talk and being loving and compassionate toward herself, no matter what.

"There will be good days and bad days, and if you make a mistake, beating yourself up is not going to help," she points out. "Self-compassion is about awareness; it's about being empathetic with one's own self. It's trying to find habits that you can enjoy and that will pull you forward."

According to Dr. Russell Barkley, a leading ADHD expert, we struggle to have "a memory of the future." What that means, Luther explains, is that it is very difficult for those with ADHD to see themselves in the future.

"We can't connect to our future selves on an emotional or intellectual level," she says. "We aren't able to think of our future selves and act from what our future selves will really, really want. It's very difficult for us to remember and act from how we want to feel and be a month from now, let alone years from now. We need multiple and constant reminders to help us manage our eating, especially when temptations arise and our willpower is worn down."

That is exactly the reason Luther suggests finding someone to be your weight loss buddy—someone who also wants to lose weight and needs support. She suggests setting short, attainable milestones like five or ten pounds at a time. She also suggests building in non-food-based celebrations to reward yourself when you reach those short goals. Other tips include getting help to manage any negative self-talk, establishing helpful structures such as lists, alarms, and reminders, and enlisting people who will be supportive—get that partner to really help you! It makes the journey more fun and helps tremendously.

Most of all, Luther says, don't think of managing your weight as a war. "Learn to be mindful and self-compassionate. And don't make weight loss your exclusive focus, either. I certainly don't want to look back on my life and see that it's been all about my weight," she states. "We need to keep it in perspective. After all, the scale doesn't tell us who we are as people!"

Chapter 17

SUCCESS IS . . . PURSUING YOUR PASSION

L aurie Dupar is on a mission—a mission to create greater awareness about ADHD for all those who have been diagnosed with the disorder and for those who are still in the dark about how their own brains work.

"I think we completely underestimate the number of people who have ADHD and the impact it has on their lives," says Dupar, a Senior Certified ADHD Coach, psychiatric mental health nurse practitioner, and co-author and editor of *The ADHD Awareness Book Project* series.

A few years ago Dupar reached a disturbing realization. "After years of working to increase the awareness of ADHD, I was concerned as to the sheer number of calls for help I was getting from people who still didn't really have a clue about it," she says.

"Too often, in the last nine years as an ADHD coach, I've met with parents, students, and newly-diagnosed adults struggling alone, not knowing that answers to their challenges were available. Many had never heard the term ADHD," Dupar notes. "They had no idea there were alternative ways to succeed by doing things that better fit their ADHD brain style."

So Dupar concluded that she just might need to shake things up a bit in order to get the information out there. "People tend to think I'm a rule follower, which I am," she says, "but if something isn't working, I'm going to find a way around it." While Dupar acknowledges that there are a lot of great people doing wonderful things regarding ADHD awareness, the word is still not reaching everyone. "We can't keep doing the same thing and expect different results."

Therefore, Dupar began sticking her neck out in order to disseminate the information she believed would help people learn about ADHD, medication, and coaching. In addition to speaking at the usual well-known ADHD conferences, she developed her own annual tele-summit, "Succeed With ADHD," inviting some of the world's leading experts to share their knowledge about ways to succeed with ADHD. She created *The ADHD Awareness Book Project* to provide people with valuable strategies and tips to help them better succeed, and to increase the awareness of ADHD worldwide. As of this writing the third book in the series is soon to be launched, and both previous books have ranked #1 on Amazon.com.

Dupar grew up without a label for her ADHD characteristics, despite the fact that other members of her family were suspected of having the condition. What's more, she says, being raised in a family with high expectations and big consequences for not meeting them created a fierce motivation for her to do well. "In a family like that, it is common for people with ADHD to hold it together and get by, because the consequences of not doing so are so great," she says.

"I was also very bright, curious, and creative, which allowed me to compensate for some of my weaknesses. Creativity helps you to be an innovative problem solver." Being naturally curious about almost everything added to Dupar's enjoyment of academics and learning. Somewhat of a perfectionist, she admits that a little Obsessive-Compulsive Disorder (OCD) was key in her ability to create calendars and structures and then follow them, taking the time to dot every "i" and cross every "t." "Living without that perfectionist tendency would have been a nightmare," she says.

In school, Dupar says she always felt like an underachiever. While she earned fairly good grades, she never thought she was living up to her potential. This is often the case among those with ADHD, who will frequently employ a strategy of creating structure by being highly active. Dupar did this, and it was common for her to have multiple extra-curricular activities going on at one time. At one point she was in the band, drill team, flag line, and playing sports all at once . . . and her biggest dilemma came on parade day, when she couldn't figure out where she needed to be!

Dupar entered college thinking she wanted to teach, but after a short semester of tutoring she changed her mind. Already in her junior year, she began to consider other ideas, ranging from business to computers, secretarial work, and psychology. Finally, she stumbled upon nursing.

"I was always interested in how the body and mind work, and academically that passion made all the difference." Dupar's grades took off and despite the late start, she ended up graduating in four years with two majors, one in psychology and one in nursing, as well as a minor in theology.

Continuing her pattern of keeping busy, Dupar studied nursing during the school year and took psychology courses in the summer. "It was my interest in the information and downright stubbornness that got me through," she says. "I was determined that this was what I was going to do."

She worked for many years as a nurse and explains how there, once again, all the structure helped. "As a nurse, you knew what you had to do minute by minute, hour by hour, and it was incredibly detailed. There are systems and structures I still use to this day that I learned in my first years as a nurse. Sometimes I wonder how I did it, but again, the consequences of not getting it right were so great that I persevered."

Meanwhile, Dupar married and began raising four children, the youngest of whom was diagnosed with ADHD at age seven. "Despite my experience and education in the medical field, I felt helpless as to how best to help him manage and overcome his challenges," she says.

Moving from the Portland, Oregon area to Sydney, Australia around the same time, Dupar was disappointed to find a lack of awareness and information on ADHD there. She struggled to figure out how to help her son succeed, which became a contributing factor in her family's decision to return to the United States a few years later.

They settled in northern California, where the scope of duty for a nurse practitioner was not the same as what Dupar had been accustomed to. "In California I would not have had the same autonomy as a nurse practitioner in Washington state," she says. These restrictions, such as the need for prescriptions to be co-signed by a psychiatrist, for example, led her to re-evaluate continuing as a nurse practitioner.

While mulling over her decision about what to do next, Dupar attended a CHADD support group meeting, still trying to find more information to help her son. The speaker that evening, Patrice Lynn, was an ADHD coach, and Dupar stayed after the meeting to talk with her.

Lynn ended up encouraging Dupar to become an ADHD coach herself, explaining how, with her background, it would be a wonderful fit. In the end Dupar agreed because the coaching profession would give her the flexibility and autonomy she wanted as a mother, and she already knew that being a nurse practitioner in California would be disappointing.

In true ADHD fashion, Dupar threw herself into pursuing her credentialing as a coach and never looked back. "It wasn't a hard decision. My goal has always been to help people pursue the life that they wanted for themselves. I am a helpless optimist." The philosophy and emerging profession of coaching was a perfect fit. Dupar says simply, "I knew it was the right decision."

"I saw what a difference coaching made in the lives of those with ADHD," she continues. "I knew I wanted to use this approach to help other parents, students, and adults overcome their ADHD challenges and feel more confident in their abilities, empowered, and successful— whatever that meant to them."

In 2002, Dupar graduated from the Coaches Training Institute, an International Coach Federation-accredited training program. Ten years later she is still as passionate about working with the ADHD population, if not more so.

"It was always about helping someone, making a difference," she explains. "It has always been about making a connection, helping people find their answers and believing in them. Sometimes it doesn't take a whole lot of information to make a big change."

Chapter 18

RESILIENCE IS KEY

"**P**eople with ADHD face challenges every day as they find ways to successfully manage the day-to-day tasks that are required to be productive in our world. Those who are resilient find ways to bounce back and achieve success," says Michael Anderson, a clinical social worker, ADHD coach, and ADDer himself.

"Even though I kept getting knocked down, I always got back up," says Anderson, who was diagnosed with ADHD at the age of 35.

Today he is passionate about helping others with ADHD find that "something" inside of themselves that will help them move forward despite the numerous failures so many of them rack up.

"You have to dig really deep and look at what is fueling your beliefs and your values. So for instance, when I try an ADHD strategy and then fail, I can look at what's getting in my way but not get stuck on it," he says. "I can think to myself, 'I know this is a product of my ADHD and I can process it.' It's not an excuse, but it does impact my values and expectations."

"It is really important to understand one's own ADHD and how it impacts you," Anderson concludes. "It's about understanding and acceptance."

Growing up with undiagnosed ADHD was extremely difficult, he admits. "It was probably the worst experience of my life. It was very difficult to know in my heart that I knew more than what my grades were showing or what people gave me credit for. And I wanted to do all these things, but couldn't pull the trigger."

"ADHD fuels frustration and anger," he continues. "It made me wonder why I could achieve in some areas and not in others. That frustration comes with a price, because you start to doubt yourself."

Anderson recalls that when he was four years old he could name all the presidents and recite numerous facts about each one of them. As he grew up he knew he was smart, but his grades were highly inconsistent—the classic telltale sign of ADHD. In math class Anderson says he could get the right answers but wasn't sure how he arrived at them, and as a result his teachers thought he was cheating.

"I got everything from As to Fs. It was difficult to sit still in class, and procrastination was a huge problem for me. But procrastination is really just a form of emotional avoidance. I didn't want to let others down, or myself. I didn't want to fail—again."

Impulsivity was another challenge for Anderson, who admits he couldn't keep his mouth shut and that this got him in a lot of difficulty both in school and out. "I was consistently getting into all kinds of trouble, and it didn't help that my father was a highly successful businessman, as well as on my town's city council." Anderson often found himself being compared to his dad, and didn't feel like he stacked up.

"People were always telling me I wasn't a good student; that I should consider a vocation rather than college," he recalls. He believed that people who knew him thought he was just a goofball and would never make it, and he found himself buying into those beliefs, dropping out of college after just one semester. "It felt like high school all over again."

Rather than give up, however, Anderson joined the military, and the structure turned out to be just what he needed. Knowing exactly what was expected of him seemed to make a big difference, and he even began taking college courses and finding success.

Before too long, he'd knocked out an associate degree and was selected for the ROTC program, giving him the opportunity to go back to college. There he earned a Bachelor's Degree in Political Science with a minor in education and military science.

Anderson, who wanted to become a military lawyer and then go into politics, earned all As in his pre-law classes, and upon graduation received a big break when he got a job with the State of Illinois. He was also selected to attend the state convention as a delegate.

"They were grooming me to run for state representative," Anderson explains. "People said I had this innate ability to understand people and their behaviors, and I probably would have been very successful, but unfortunately my impatience and impulsivity got in the way." Anderson says that after running into a few hurdles, he walked away rather than working with the situation, "probably my biggest regret in life."

Instead, he took a teaching job in Naperville, 35 miles west of Chicago, working with disabled children. He enjoyed that environment, and met his first wife at the school where he taught. It was his wife (who had been involved in the special education field for a long time) who suggested that Anderson might have ADHD.

Anderson agreed to check it out and, after seeing a local psychologist, was formally diagnosed. "I thought, 'Okay, I'll learn how to make a to-do list and my world will be better,'" he recalls. He also began taking ADHD medication, and says that by the end of the first day he was freaked out by how much he had accomplished. "I thought, 'This is pretty cool.' I thought I was cured."

But life just doesn't work that way, Anderson soon realized. A short time later he'd grown tired of people checking up on him, asking if he was taking his medication and if he was practicing his strategies. So he simply stopped doing both. As a result, his challenges with patience and impulsivity returned, big time. He also recalls that he was no longer able to be as productive as he had been while taking medication.

He had, however, found success working with handicapped students, so he began to consider attending graduate school to earn a master's degree in clinical social work. Once he made that decision and was accepted he wanted to do well, so he was motivated to go back and seriously look into "this whole ADHD thing. I can remember spending hours in the library reading about ADHD. I would just dig and dig and dig."

Anderson was so serious about finding a way to deal with his ADHD that he flew from Illinois to California to meet with Dr. Daniel Amen at the world-renowned Amen Clinic in San Francisco. The clinic performs and evaluates brain scans utilizing high-resolution brain SPECT imaging (a widely accepted nuclear medicine procedure) to provide objective diagnostic information. At the clinic, Anderson learned a lot more about his ADHD and began taking his medication once again.

"I knew that knowledge was not necessarily power unless you put it to use," he says. "As a result, I wanted to learn everything I could about ADHD and what I could do about it." He also attended the CHADD conference that year and met David Giwerc, the founder of the ADD Coach Academy. "This opened up a whole new world about ADHD and what was going on with me," Anderson says.

He began working with an ADHD coach and was able to earn a 3.8 grade point average in graduate school, eventually earning his LSCW and loving the work he did to develop a recovery program for men transitioning into the real world from treatment services for issues such as post-traumatic stress disorder.

Anderson got his own ADHD coaching certificate a few years later and began coaching full time until 2011, when he was hired by the United States Army to work at Fort Leonard Wood, Missouri, to do mental health and substance abuse work with troops returning from Iraq and Afghanistan.

Today Anderson loves his career, and at times still finds it hard to believe that he was selected to do what he does. "I can't even describe how it felt when the job was offered to me," he says. "I was so proud of myself. I think I had begun to feel more confident internally, but this gave me the external validation I needed. I'm not that screw-up everyone thought I was, and I'm working with a part of the population that is really difficult to work with, just loving it."

Anderson says that his life began to come together when he started to focus not so much on his to-do list, but on himself—and on learning that success with ADHD is not about *not* having problems. It's not about forgetting to pick something up, or about dealing (or refusing to deal) with your procrastination. "You can have the best systems in the world," he says, "but if you don't understand what's going on and accept your whole self, your strengths and weaknesses combined, it's not going to work. There will be relapses and mistakes made, but you have to embrace that. You have to understand what is getting in the way and then move on."

"I wish ADHD was as simple as attention disregulation, procrastination, and forgetfulness," Anderson says. "I wish it was that easy and you could just take a pill to alleviate those challenges, but being undiagnosed leads to a whole host of other issues. It impacts your whole being, your self-esteem. You make judgments about who you are and how you perform, and that in turn impacts your behavior. That is far more detrimental than the fact that you have difficulty paying attention and can't remember to bring your book to class."

Mark Twain said, "The inability to forget is infinitely more devastating than the inability to remember," which Anderson considers a great touchstone. "Those of us with ADHD work so hard to remember things, yet our inability to forget our mistakes is exponentially more difficult." He also likes to quote Dr. Russell Ramsey, who says, "Effective coping for adult ADHD is not defined by the absence of problems, but by having ways to understand and manage them."

Anderson urges those with ADHD to stop hyper-focusing on finding the right strategy to "fix" their problems, focusing instead on learning to manage and accept them. "Most importantly, what we all need to do is embrace and accept our authentic selves," he states. "That acceptance includes failures and successes, but without dwelling on the failures."

"It's not surprising that pessimistic, automatic negative thoughts and negative assumptions about one's abilities are common with ADDers," he continues, "but it's those negative thoughts and perceptions that interfere with the implementation of effective coping strategies. These maladaptive thoughts diminish one's ability to take proactive steps to change one's circumstances."

Anderson emphasizes the need to learn how to manage one's expectations, which is what builds resiliency. Resiliency is one of the integral components necessary to improve functioning and performance despite having ADHD.

It's not easy, Anderson admits, knowing how long he has struggled with self-acceptance. But he also knows the price you pay if you don't allow yourself to forgive and move on with your life.

Chapter 19

PAINTING MAKES HIS HEART SING

Fifteen years ago, Duane Gordon was about to lose yet another job. His marriage was on the rocks. "I was a lousy husband and father," he admits.

Flash forward to today and Gordon, who was officially diagnosed with ADHD in 1998, can now boast not only of keeping his job, but of rising rapidly through the ranks and consistently landing on his feet through four mergers and acquisitions at the same Montreal company over a span of 15 years. No longer estranged, it was his wife who suggested he tell his story for this book. He has a good relationship with his two grown daughters. On top of that, he has rediscovered his love for painting and carves out about 20 hours worth of studio time each week.

So how did this Canadian native turn his life around? Discovering that he had ADHD at the age of 33, and ultimately working with an ADHD coach, helped Gordon create a more productive, happier, successful life for himself and his family.

As a youngster, his undiagnosed ADHD didn't prove too much of a problem because his family moved around the world, living in more than 23 different places while he was growing up. "As weird as it sounds, that was an advantage. I never had a chance to get bored,"

Gordon says. He managed to get good grades in school even though he never studied—although he admits that nearly every report card contained statements to the effect that he was not living up to his potential, he didn't pay attention, and he often disrupted the class. Despite these problems, Gordon made it through school fairly easily due to his native intelligence.

Life became much more difficult, however, when he entered the military through the Collège Militaire Royal in St. Jean, Quebec. It certainly was not the school he wanted to attend. Always passionate about art, Gordon won a scholarship to the prestigious Banff School of Fine Arts in Alberta the summer after his high school graduation, but his father refused to allow him to go. Gordon says, "My father felt I'd be wasting my life pursuing art. He told me, 'You're going to military college, you'll get a career, and when you've done that, if you still want to paint, then you can pursue art.'"

At the Collège Militaire, Gordon found himself perpetually in trouble of one kind or another. Failing classes when he could no longer get by without studying, and always on extra duty for one transgression or another, his situation grew steadily worse. "I wasn't trying to cause trouble," Gordon insists. "I wasn't a rebel. But there were rules like you wouldn't believe, and I was always forgetting stuff. The older I got, the worse it became. Life just gets more complicated. As a child, you have your parents telling you what to do. In school, you have your teachers telling you what to do. But once you are on your own, it all falls apart. At least it definitely did for me."

Gordon managed to graduate from military college and, shortly thereafter, left the military altogether. But trouble continued to nip at his heels as he realized he couldn't hold a job. "I will say one thing for the military," he says. "When you have ADHD, that much structure in your life can be a big help. Once I returned to civilian life, I wouldn't follow directions. I would yell at my bosses and get fired, or get bored and quit." Married by now, with two young daughters as well as personal and financial commitments, Gordon admits that his behavior during this time period "drove my wife insane."

For example, in 1988 Gordon flew to Newfoundland for a friend's wedding and, while there, applied for a teaching job at a local college without consulting his wife. He got the job, and returned home just long enough to help pack up their belongings and move clear across the continent. Eight years later—which was actually a record for Gordon—he decided to switch gears once again, this time to become a computer programmer. Again the bags were packed, and the family returned to Montreal. "My wife agreed that time only because her family was living in Montreal, and she was happy to be returning home," Gordon says.

Surprisingly, all went well in his new job. Too well, in fact, because soon Gordon was promoted to a managerial position. Once again, he found himself at risk of being fired. "I could barely manage myself, let alone be in a management position."

Luckily, however, Gordon finally figured out he had ADHD when his six-year-old daughter was diagnosed with it. He and his wife both read *Driven to Distraction* to understand what their daughter was living with. Gordon recalls, "We immediately recognized my symptoms in what the book was describing, perhaps even more so than my daughter's symptoms. After all, she was just getting started."

Once Gordon was officially diagnosed, he began taking Ritalin. It helped, but didn't solve the problem. "We always say that 'pills don't give skills,'" he remarks, "and I'm a prime example of that."

Knowing that ADHD was the cause of his problems was a big help, but this purely intellectual understanding didn't actually solve them. With his job in jeopardy and his marriage tenuous, Gordon decided to apply for a study he had seen advertised in the local newspaper, about the effects of training and coaching on people with ADHD.

It was expensive. He had to undergo extensive testing and be rediagnosed. Once accepted, he had to attend classes which, while educational, didn't seem to change much for him. He still found he was unable to apply what he had learned to his life. Finally at his wits' end, Gordon visited the psychologist heading up the study and asked him if he was crazy. "I don't know what to do," he told the doctor. "Nothing is working!"

Assuring Gordon he wasn't crazy, the psychologist recommended that he hire an ADHD coach. The results, he says, were phenomenal. "It was really just taking the stuff I'd learned and putting it into practice in a step-by-step way," Gordon remembers. "But the effects that it had on my life were profound."

Gordon went back to work and explained to his boss about his ADHD, agreeing to take a demotion and the pay cut that went along with it. But due to the work he did with his coach to improve his on-the-job performance, he was able to earn back his old salary (and more) in under three months, along with a promotion to a more senior technical position rather than one in management.

Gordon also found that with coaching, he was able to create systems to better manage his finances. His relationship with his wife soon flourished, as he was able to become a responsible, reliable partner instead of one "extra kid" his wife had to care for. Working with his coach, Gordon soon began to recognize his strengths and weaknesses. He learned to use his strengths more and to avoid, delegate, or manage the tasks that incorporated his weaknesses, so they would no longer be such obstacles to his success.

"My life before and after coaching is like the difference between night and day," Gordon says. "It's not a panacea, and it's not easy, but there are ways for you to really turn your life around if you want."

In addition, Gordon is now a successful artist. He had completely given up art on that fateful day when his father sent him off to military college. It was his wife who, after noticing him drawing animals at his daughters' request, surprised him with drawing classes as a Christmas present. She hadn't known about his artistic talents, Gordon says. "I remember her asking me, 'Did you know you could draw like that?' before I explained why I'd given up art. After much hesitation, I went to the drawing class . . . and then never looked back."

Gordon, who has had numerous exhibitions and shows over the last few years, says he thrives on the rush of ideas. He believes his ADHD probably plays a role in his mental hyperactivity. "For me the ideas have always come so fast, I'm overwhelmed by them. In fact, I will never live long enough to paint all the ideas I've already had," he confides.

But ideas aren't enough, Gordon continues. "It's not the ideas people appreciate. Every ADDer can vouch for the number of ideas we have that never become reality. You have to *create* something from your ideas. That means you have to carve out time in your schedule. You have to stop procrastinating. You have to get your paint and your brushes and get your butt in the studio. You have to get started, and then you have to keep at it until you're finished. There's work to be done if you're going to create anything," he says.

On weekends Gordon is in his studio at 7:00 a.m., and during the week he goes there as soon as he gets home from work and grabs a quick bite to eat. "Believe me, I have every excuse in the world not to make time for my art," he says. "I have a full time job, I have a wife and kids—there are lots and lots of reasons not to do this. It would be so easy to let my ADHD take control. It would be so easy to procrastinate or watch television, or give in to that voice that says I don't feel like painting tonight."

But by now Gordon has learned how to manage his ADHD. He has learned to appreciate its gifts and to overcome the struggles it brings. Returning to his painting is just the icing on the cake. "I have a great life now," he says. "And painting makes my soul sing."

Chapter 20

A JOURNEY OF SELF-DISCOVERY

"'Mom, you seem so happy,' my 26-year-old son said to me the other day. And I am," Sheryl Greenfield says, smiling. "But I wasn't always." At age 55, Sheryl has finally discovered what it means to trust herself, to believe in herself, and to be her own cheerleader.

"It wasn't easy," Greenfield says, looking back on her journey of self-discovery. "I grew up feeling broken, like I never fit in. It took me more than 50 years to find my voice, but I finally did, and it feels amazing!"

Greenfield's ADHD was not diagnosed until she was well into adulthood. She grew up in the suburbs of Philadelphia in a family that looked perfect from the outside, but was not so flawless on the inside. "In our family, it was all about appearances," she explains. Keeping up the façade was so demanding that by sixth grade Greenfield was seeing a psychiatrist. She was overweight, dealing with a lot of insecurities, and (yes, the old standard) "not working up to her potential."

"I was so embarrassed to be in therapy, I would sneak home from school and hide out in the bathroom before appointments," she says. "I never said one word to the psychiatrist during the entire year and a half I was seeing her." Her mother tried putting her in group therapy, but that wasn't much better. "I still didn't participate. I was totally shut down."

About school, Greenfield says, "Reading was always very difficult for me. I couldn't concentrate, and while I was good at certain things, I did very poorly in others. I tried glossing over my struggles, lying about my grades, even though my parents always found out. I had low self-esteem and I was very frustrated. But at home I had learned that the important thing was to hide my problems behind a beautiful smile so no one would know how unhappy I was or how much pain I was in."

"Because I had so little self-confidence, I did whatever my mother told me to do," Greenfield says. Her mother encouraged her to study interior design because she was artistic. "Her plan for my life was simple: go to college, get a degree, work until you find a husband, and then raise a family."

She talks about how difficult the first part of this "plan" was for her. "The pressure for me in college was unbelievable. I felt I had to work ten times as hard as anyone else. If I loved what I was doing, I would do well. I aced economics, but always had poor marks in other subjects. I was shocked when I managed to graduate." Even then, although she had her degree, Greenfield recalls that she never had the confidence to look for a job in interior design. "I worked as a waitress and then as a bank teller until I met my husband, Bruce."

"Having children only made things worse," she continues. "I'd felt like a failure most of my life, but I thought surely I would succeed as a mother. After all, it's a so-called maternal 'instinct,' right?" But her state of mind went further downhill from there, Greenfield admits. She found she was bored with her young children and wondered what was wrong with her, always thinking, "What a terrible mother I must be!"

But once again she hid her true feelings. After all, how could she admit not liking motherhood? "Everyone thought I had the perfect life," she says. "I was the president of the PTA, served on a variety of boards, and always looked well-put-together. The house was always clean and organized, but only because I had a housekeeper—of course, I felt guilty I couldn't handle that myself. I enjoyed entertaining and throwing parties because of the stimulation . . . but do you know how much energy that took? And when we went on vacations, for me, something as seemingly simple as packing a suitcase was overwhelming."

Stressed with the effort to keep up appearances, Greenfield was miserable, dealing with bottled-up anger, anxiety, and feelings of hopelessness. While in her 30s she again sought the help of a therapist, who prescribed anti-depressants. These took the edge off, but were not the solution. "I screamed a lot back then," she admits, remembering those days tearfully. "I would lose the kids' papers for school. I just couldn't keep it together." She is quick to credit her husband for helping her get through that period of her life. "He is so even-keeled, he picked up all the loose ends and never made me feel bad about it."

Things became even more difficult for Greenfield when her oldest son Josh was diagnosed with ADHD at the age of seven. He was unable to sit still for one minute. "I knew something was wrong," she says. "From the time he was little, I knew he was different and that he struggled like me in many ways." We had him tested and it confirmed what I had known all along."

From that point on, Greenfield fought hard for Josh to get the accommodations at school that would help him succeed. He also began taking Ritalin, and went from barely scraping through school to earning straight As. It wasn't a perfect solution, Greenfield admits, because on the down side, Ritalin quieted her son's exuberant personality. But today Josh is a very successful musician, as well as a chef in the catering business he owns along with his younger brother Michael.

"He's worked very hard on himself," Greenfield says proudly of her son. Josh graduated with a degree in marketing from the University of Delaware, but went to New York to follow his dream of making it with his rock band. "We encouraged him to follow his passion," she says.

Once Josh was diagnosed with ADHD, Greenfield became sure she had it, too. One day she tried his medication. "For the first time, I could sit and read a book and really focus," she says. Shortly after this, Sheryl was diagnosed with ADHD as well. "Honestly, at first," she confesses, "I didn't really read much about my ADHD. I would merely use it as an excuse, blaming my lack of organization on it. But a friend of mine suggested I read her sister-in-law Sari Solden's new book, *Women and Attention Deficit Disorder*."

"That was five years ago now. When I read Sari's book, followed by Lara Honos-Webb's *The Gift of Adult ADD*, my eyes were finally opened. Now I realize that I'm not screwed up. I have strengths. I have a voice." This epiphany eventually led Greenfield to want to use what she'd learned to help others who have struggled in the same ways that she has. She spoke to a therapist friend. "My friend told me that I could help her run some support groups, but first I had to become more knowledgeable. 'Go and learn,' she said to me."

So Greenfield did just that, and in her search for more information, she discovered David Giwerc and the ADD Coach Academy. "When I first listened to his online video, I cried from the moment he started talking until he stopped," she says. "What he was saying hit my heart. This man is talking about me! I've *got* to sign up for this."

Unbeknownst to Greenfield, this was not the end of her story— merely the beginning. Taking classes through ADDCA, she not only learned how to help others but to help herself as well. "For nearly four months I was sick in bed," she says. "I wasn't physically ill. I was deal-ing with a lot of emotions. A lot of that old stuff—regrets, self-judgment, mourning, and so on—was coming up, and I had to learn how to let it go. I cried a lot."

Greenfield had begun to do what she calls "the work." She re-lates, "I remember David Giwerc telling me that he could only take me so far. 'You have to be the one to believe in yourself,' he said to me." Working with Giwerc as her mentor coach, together they pushed through Greenfield's walls, and she began to discover who she really was.

She recalls how things came to a head, however, during an ADDCA conference she and Giwerc both attended. He realized that Greenfield had not fully developed her self-confidence and independence—that he had become her surrogate decision-maker. She explains, "I had put him on a pedestal and needed to learn how to trust myself." Knowing how important this step was for Greenfield's development as a coach, not to mention as a confident adult with or without ADHD, Giwerc withdrew from her during those days at the conference.

"It was really tough for me when David wasn't there for me, but I knew from the beginning I was learning something important from this. And as hard as it was, I have come out of it stronger," Greenfield says. "I have so much more confidence in myself." Today she is grateful to Giwerc for what he did, and their friendship is stronger than ever.

Greenfield is now working as an ADHD coach herself, and wants to help others find their own inner voices. She has also developed a wonderful relationship with her own children, and has brought her new confidence in her ability to relate to young people into her career. She particularly enjoys working with young men and women about to go to college and their families, knowing the struggles that those with ADHD have during this important time in their lives.

"The most important lesson I learned is to trust myself, to believe in myself," Greenfield says. "It's nice when people notice my transformation or all the hard work I have done to get where I am today, but I no longer need the confirmation of others because I know it inside, in my heart."

"I'm comfortable in my own skin now," she continues. "I feel good about myself. I'm content. No, it's not easy. I still work very hard every day. My ADD is not going away, but now I know how to manage it. Things still come up, but I don't let them immobilize me. I get out of bed every day asking myself, 'How can I make a difference today?'"

Chapter 21

TRANSITIONING FROM HIGH SCHOOL TO COLLEGE WITH ADHD

Transitioning from high school to college is never easy, but for people with ADHD it can be a nightmare. The good news, however, is that it doesn't have to be that way. For Anthony Robertson, 27, who now works as the lead Systems Engineer for the F-16 program at Wright-Patterson Air Force Base in Dayton, Ohio, getting as much help as possible was crucial.

"Sure, I wanted to do it on my own, but I soon realized it's okay to ask for help," Robertson says. "Why not ask for accommodations if it will make your life easier?"

Diagnosed with ADHD and dyslexia early on, he encountered his most difficult struggles in middle school, but once he got the help he needed, Robertson went from failing most of his classes in seventh grade to getting all As and Bs in eighth grade and beyond. Reading always took him a lot longer than most of his peers, he says, and being given more time to take tests or turn in assignments made a big difference for him.

Robertson's transition from high school to college was made easier because his counselors in high school connected him with people who could help him in college. While it did take him five years to graduate from the University of Kentucky with a degree in mechanical engineering and a minor in mathematics, he went on to earn a Master's Degree in Aeronautical and Astronautical Engineering from Purdue University in Chicago. To reach these goals, Robertson continued to rely on accommodations to help him compensate for the challenges of his ADHD.

He says that his first two years in college were the most difficult because he needed to take general courses to meet the basic requirements, but once he could concentrate on his core engineering classes, where his true passions lay, he was able to earn mostly As. "It was the goal that motivated me to get through no matter what," he recalls, typifying the way in which, for people with ADHD, being interested in a subject commonly makes it much easier to focus and do the work. Robertson attributes his early interest in engineering to his grandfather, a World War II pilot. "That's most likely the reason I fell in love with airplanes," he says. "I just always thought they were awesome."

Robertson also credits his success in college to being the project manager of the University of Kentucky's solar-powered car team. "Get involved in extracurricular activities," he advises emphatically. "In school, my priorities were: number one, solar-powered car team; two, school; and three, a social life." He admits that he didn't often have time for number three, but the girl he was dating at the time, now his wife, would come to the garage to study just so she could see him.

Twenty-four-year-old Neel Kanth Sawhney is also a firm believer in asking for help. Sawhney, also diagnosed with ADHD while in middle school, says that his job in his college's disability office really helped him view his own ADHD differently. "It was very educational for me. That's when I started to think of ADHD differently. Rather than try to hide it and drag my feet, I began to look at how people can use their disabilities to their advantage."

Sawhney, who graduated from the School of Visual Arts (SVA) in New York City and now attends Columbia University as a post-baccalaureate student, gives the example of various famous artists and writers who may have had to deal with depression, anxiety, or OCD but whose creative work, as a result, seems extremely powerful. He likes to think ADHD contributes to his own creativity in the same way.

Sawhney also recalls how working in the disability office taught him how easy it is to resolve problems when you ask for accommodations. "If you have ADD or depression or dyslexia, you can get extra time to take tests or finish school work. Working with a tutor or coming in and talking to someone in the disability office, you can create a plan that will help you achieve your goals."

Sawhney explains that while many of his own problems center on a lack of focus, poor organizational skills, and procrastination, no one really addressed his ADHD prior to his enrollment at SVA. He realizes now that he should have advocated for himself earlier on, and that he could have benefited from all the accommodations available to those with his condition.

Now, however, Sawhney is determined to do his best and get the help he needs in order to achieve his goals. Interested in psychiatry, he says that he is applying to several post-baccalaureate premedical programs, with an eye toward eventually going on to medical school.

Someday Sawhney would also like to write self-help books for young people with disabilities. He believes that if you approach kids at an early age, providing them with an understanding of their disabilities as well as giving them the right tools and strategies, they will be better prepared for the future.

In his continuing efforts to help others with disabilities, Sawhney sits on the board of a developing non-profit group named Health Works NY that aims to bring educational health awareness programs to the working population, students, and unpaid caregivers. Sawhney grows quite passionate when explaining how one program he is working on will address awareness around depression and anxiety and is aimed at helping students learn how stress directly affects the mind and body. He hopes that programs such as these will help others learn how to take control of their lives.

"I suppose this is my way of trying to make an impact on the world, no matter how small it may be, so that those who struggle with disabilities can lead better lives."

Sawhney admits that he didn't do very well in school until reaching SVA. He feels he could have done better if he had applied himself, but wasn't sure how to do that. When he made the switch from a community college to SVA, however, he decided he would not settle for less than his best. "I can either go down the dark road, or get all the As I can," he remembers thinking to himself. "People will surprise themselves if they just create their own support systems. And once you get one A, whenever you doubt yourself, you just go back to that A, to that positive reinforcement. Whatever you have done right before, you know you can do it again. Success builds more success."

"Self-esteem was one of the biggest things for me," Sawhney admits. "If you don't have the right tools, then you're going to keep making mistakes and feeling badly about it." Now he says he works hard not to beat himself up. "There are always going to be bumps in life, but when I hit one of those bumps, I just keep going. I don't want one bump to turn into three bumps."

Twenty-four-year-old Kyle Dopfel was not diagnosed with ADHD until her second year at Duke University in Durham, North Carolina. "For me, just learning more about the disorder and understanding how it affected me felt like half the battle," she says. "Suddenly a lot of things about me made more sense and because I was aware of it, I could then identify times when it might come into play and avoid further problems arising."

Dopfel admits that she struggled around her diagnosis, having trouble accepting it. She says she has always been a bit skeptical of ADHD diagnoses, her perception being that the condition is over-diagnosed and is often either an excuse or a way to obtain an unfair advantage.

Once she "came around," accepted what she had, and pursued treatment in the form of both medication and therapy, Dopfel was amazed at the good it did her. "It wasn't that I hadn't been able to achieve some degree of success previously, but it had been an extreme struggle. I had been dealing with a huge obstacle without even realizing it was there. Treatment didn't just improve my academic performance, but also made a huge difference for me in pretty much every aspect of my life," she says. "I began to feel happier, lighter, and able to go through life and get things done without nearly the difficulty I'd had before, or the stress and frustration."

Fittingly, Dopfel's work now centers almost wholly around ADHD. After graduation, she worked with the ADHD Corrections Project at the Delaware Center for Justice, a position she obtained through AmeriCorps Vista. The project also received additional funding from ADDA. Recently, Dopfel was hired by ADDA to continue her work with the ADHD Corrections Project, developing a national program for ADHD based on her work with the Delaware pilot project.

"This is a pilot reentry initiative which aims to identify inmates with undiagnosed or untreated ADHD and to help them be as successful as possible by preparing them for their release and connecting them with all of the necessary support services in their communities," Dopfel explains.

"What I have learned is that brains with ADHD don't necessarily function any better or worse than brains without ADHD—people with ADHD are no more or less intelligent. Brains with ADHD just happen to function *differently* than those without. I would recommend that people with ADHD avoid thinking of it as a flaw and try not to be discouraged by it. They can be just as successful as anyone else, if not more so. People with ADHD are often some of the most creative, innovative, and inspired people because of the way they process their thoughts and ideas."

Or, as Anthony Robertson succinctly sums it up, "You just have to believe in yourself."

Here are some tips for high school students with ADHD who are transferring to college:

- Be comfortable with your ADHD diagnosis. Don't be afraid to acknowledge your condition—it's not your fault or something to be ashamed of. Your brain simply works differently. Not worse, just *differently*.

- <u>Become familiar with your college disability services office</u>. It can help you a great deal—probably more than you think. So seek out the accommodations available to you there.

- <u>Acknowledge your strengths and your areas of need</u>. This will hone your abilities to self-assess, self-strategize, problem solve, and—as a result—self-manage.

- <u>Practice lifestyle habits for success</u>. Eat right. Exercise. Get enough sleep. Establishing patterns of daily living and successfully tending to basic details of eating, sleeping, and exercising can be tremendously empowering.

- <u>Read college success stories</u>. Learn what has worked for others and consider whether or not their tools and strategies might work for you.

- <u>Understand student responsibilities</u>. Know what is expected of you before you actually start college.

- <u>Participate in pre-college visits</u>. It is important to learn whether or not the college you choose is a good fit for you and what kinds of resources it has for someone with ADHD.

- <u>Develop good study skills</u>. Waiting until the night before to study for a test or write a term paper is not going to work in college. Learn how to overcome procrastination. Figure out what works for you—is it finding a quiet place to study, using headphones to block out noise distractions, or making sure to exercise first in order to be more focused?

- <u>Utilize peer tutor services</u>. Colleges offer a range of support services that include editors and tutors who can assist you with assignments and papers, and supplementary instruction or reinforcement of subject matter.

- <u>Self-advocate</u>. Teachers are unaware that a student suffers from ADHD and instead may misattribute poor academic performance to a lack of effort. Talk to your professors and speak up about accommodations such as needing extra time on tests, or sitting by the door so that you can quietly leave and walk around for a few minutes without bothering the class.

- <u>Take responsibility for your own education</u>. The key to securing the right accommodations for yourself is your own self-knowledge and acceptance of your ADHD. Learn how your disability affects you in school and how best to minimize the impacts. It is up to you!

Chapter 22

ATTITUDE IS A DECISION

"The remarkable thing is we have a choice every day regarding the attitude we will embrace for that day. We cannot change our past . . . we cannot change the fact that people will act a certain way. We cannot change the inevitable. The only thing we can do is play on the one string we have, and that is our attitude . . . I am convinced that life is 10 percent what happens to me and 90 percent how I react to it . . . As so it is with all of us. We are in charge of our attitudes." —Preacher and author Charles Swindoll

"Attitude is a decision," says Bob Madonna, Principal and Executive Vice President of Sales and Marketing for McCoy Enterprises, as well as Partner and CEO of Making Music for Families, a music educational program for infants and children through the age of five.

"No matter what the setback, I've been able to keep being positive," says Madonna, who also has ADHD. Though he has had his share of struggles, failures, and disappointments, Madonna explains that no matter what, rather than feeling sorry for himself, he simply keeps going. He feels blessed for all he does have, and says that this positive attitude, coupled with taking the time to plan, is the secret of his success.

Madonna was not officially diagnosed with ADHD until his 40s, and admits that 20 years later he still has problems with interrupting, procrastination, not listening, daydreaming, leg-thumping, the need for constant brain stimulation, and a smattering of OCD. Of those issues, he says, "They don't go away, but you can deal with them so that they don't get in your way. Attitude is about focusing on what we can control, which is us—our emotions, what we say, and how we say it."

As a youngster, Madonna says he was the kind of student who just got by. "I never studied, and if you needed to get a 70 to pass, I got a 71."

He attended Catholic school, where he explains that you sat with hands folded while a teacher or nun spoke. "School was very structured, and that meant most of my day was spent daydreaming, looking out the window or thinking about what I was going to do when I got home. I did everything but listen."

When Madonna graduated from high school he says he planned to join the Marines, but his future in-laws convinced him to give community college a try. "I figured, why not?" he says. "I didn't have anything else to do." He surprised everyone—including himself—when he ended up on the Dean's List every semester.

A history major at first, Madonna hated that and switched to business, earning an associate's degree before getting a job with Bell of Pennsylvania. Then, at the company's expense, he took classes at night and graduated from Widener University in Chester, Pennsylvania with a Bachelor's Degree in Business.

Madonna worked at Bell Atlantic for 23 years, during which time he held 18 different positions, working at everything from marketing, sales, product management, computers, operations, and training. "I did it all, " he says. "It was fantastic. For my brain it was great—the variety, and having to constantly learn new things."

After leaving Bell Atlantic in 1996, Madonna was the Executive Vice President of Sales and Marketing for NumereX, and then ran four different companies in five years, never sitting in the same office for very long.

"Because of the way my brain works, I need constant stimulation," he says. "If I don't have enough things on the table, I get bored and lazy." He tells others with ADHD that variety is essential for their brains, either in what they do or the roles they play.

Madonna says he has learned a variety of ways to keep himself organized, the most important of which is list-making. He admits, however, that details are not his strong suit and talks about how vital it is for those with ADHD to recognize their limits. "It's important that people with ADD understand areas where other people can complement them."

Getting diagnosed, Madonna says, has allowed him to understand how his brain works, to figure out what makes him tick. It has also given him the confidence to tell people he has ADHD and, as a result, to explain to his colleagues what he needs. "I tell them up front that I make decisions quickly, I don't like a long story, I just want to get to the bottom line. I can do that now without feeling guilty or being ashamed."

The most important thing that those with ADHD can do, he says, is to take stock of their strengths and weaknesses and find those who can help out in the areas where they are not as strong.

For Madonna, having a lot of balls in the air is what keeps him happy. While he has sat on the boards of many non-profit organizations, he recognizes that many of those with ADHD may not have the variety he has had in his work life. He thus urges them to include volunteerism in their lives, explaining that it can be a wonderful way to find that variety.

However, for Madonna, ultimately it all comes back to attitude. "I will not allow my life to be negatively impacted by things or people that are beyond my control," he says. "I will not take years off my life by allowing myself to become frustrated, aggravated, or upset over situations, rules, or other minutiae over which I have no control. I will look to focus on what I control in a professional positive manner."

Chapter 23

ATTENDING AN ADHD CONFERENCE FELT LIKE COMING HOME

Terry Matlen says that her ADHD diagnosis was life-changing.

"It filled in all the blanks for me," she explains. "Why I couldn't keep a tidy house, why I procrastinated, why it was so hard for me to put a dinner together that would make my family happy, why I struggled so with paperwork."

Matlen, a psychotherapist, writer, and coach specializing in adult attention deficit issues, wasn't diagnosed until her early 40s, nearly 20 years ago. "My own ADHD journey began while trying to help my daughter," she says. "As a toddler she was so hyperactive that it took two adults at all times to care for her."

Matlen, whose own form of ADHD is the inattentive type, says, "I'm slow and quiet and dreamy, while my daughter was all over the place. So out of a desperate need to try to figure out how to help my child, I began to read everything I could on ADHD."

This was back in the late '80s and early '90s, when there was very little information available on the subject, so information was difficult for Matlen to find. "But somehow I found a book on adult ADHD, and out of curiosity began to read and identify different family members that I thought might have it. Still, the connection wasn't there that I might have ADHD as well," she admits. "But slowly after time, it all came together—my growing up and why things were the way they were. Toward the end of the book, I began to think, 'Maybe that's me.'"

Matlen then read *I'm Not Lazy, Stupid or Crazy?!* by Kate Kelly and Peggy Ramundo, and began to see how ADHD could explain her own difficulties. "These books were answering questions I'd had for a long time."

Next, she attended an ADHD conference held in nearby Ann Arbor, Michigan to not only learn more about the condition for her daughter's sake, "but to help me figure out what was going on with me."

Returning home from that conference, Matlen decided it was time to find out for sure, and went to see a local psychologist who specialized in adult ADHD. He confirmed that she did indeed have it.

"To be honest, it took me awhile to accept my ADHD diagnosis, though," says Matlen, who went for second and third opinions and was still in denial. She continued to tell herself that her problems were the result of a character weakness on her part. At times she believed that maybe she really was just lazy, or a bad mother because she couldn't sit and play a board game with her kids. Perhaps it was more than a brain disorder—perhaps she was just selfish.

"It took a lot of exploring with professionals, reading, and studying to get to that point of acceptance," says Matlen, who was also very moved by reading Sari Solden's book *Women with Attention Deficit Disorder*. "That book is what really sealed the deal for me and helped me move forward as a woman with ADHD, both personally and professionally. And once I came to terms with that concept, I didn't experience the grief that some do, or become depressed. I wasn't upset about all those years that were lost to me. I took my diagnosis and ran."

Growing up, Matlen said she had no clue as to what her difficulties were. She was actually a very good student in her elementary school years and liked to learn. She had lots of friends and wasn't a troublemaker, but more the quiet, sensitive soul. She was kind-hearted and would reach out to other children who were having problems.

"It didn't affect me too much until my family moved from Detroit to the suburbs when I was in the sixth grade and everything blew up," Matlen says.

Schools in the suburbs placed a greater emphasis on academics, and she found she could no longer get by without studying or doing homework. At home the parental supervision wasn't there because Matlen's father had died an early death a few years earlier, and her mother was busy trying to support and raise three young children on her own.

"Middle school was a total disaster," Matlen says, admitting she didn't do well academically or fit in socially. "My self-esteem plummeted."

She continued to struggle until near the end of her high school years, when she found her niche in the music, art, and English departments. "I was very artistic and musical and began to excel in those areas," she says. "I started connecting with the artsy kids, and being children of the '60s and '70s, we formed bands and would go out and perform. I also took as many art classes as I possibly could."

Senior year came, however, and as the other kids began to plan for graduation Matlen was still in day-to-day survival mode. "I had no idea what I was going to do," she says. When her best friend applied for college she figured she would, too, but then didn't get in.

Thankfully, Matlen's friend's mother stepped in, "perhaps recognizing my situation. She called the local university and asked them to give me a chance and they did!" Pursuing art, Matlen began to thrive in an academic setting for the first time since elementary school.

She received a Bachelor of Arts Degree in Art Education, but when she discovered teaching wasn't a good fit she continued with school, earning her Masters in Clinical Social Work at Wayne State University in Detroit. Matlen was even awarded two graduate school scholarships which the university gave to its top undergraduate students.

"I was always drawn to the inner world of our minds and what makes people tick, "she says, and while the amount of paperwork was tremendous, she persevered because she had found her passion. "Like I tell my clients, find your passion and follow it."

Following graduation, Matlen got a job working with young adults in an outpatient psychiatric clinic. Most of the patients had been hospitalized and needed follow-up psychiatric treatment.

Later, Matlen married and started a family. In the '90s she opened a private practice working solely with adults with ADHD, but found it difficult to concentrate on her business while simultaneously fielding phone calls from the school about her special-needs daughter who was dealing with challenges of her own.

Deciding that it would be beneficial for her and her family if she worked out of her home, Matlen began to do more online work and started the website www.ADDConsults.com. She also founded and still moderates the first and largest international listserv serving ADHD professionals.

Around this same time, Matlen became interested in coaching and studied with life coach Nancy Ratey, who mentored her in the field. She became credentialed through The Institute for the Advancement of ADHD Coaching (IAAC). Her work today, however, is geared more toward consulting, writing, and presenting.

Matlen has an online group coaching program called the ADD Action Team (www.ADDactionTeam.com), which she offers at an affordable price because of her belief that everyone should be able to seek coaching support. She also occasionally works with pharmaceutical companies, writing articles and participating in educational programs. She was one of the ADHD experts at Shire's "ADHD Experts on Call" program (along with Ty Pennington), which ran for a number of years out of New York City.

These days Matlen frequently contributes articles to *ADDitude Magazine*, is a guest on various ADD podcasts, and is interviewed for and quoted frequently in articles at PsychCentral.com. She also co-founded the Virtual ADHD Conference and the popular website www.WomenWithADHD.com.

Matlen is the author of the book *Survival Tips for Women with ADHD*, and is currently writing a second book on women with ADHD, to be published in 2014 through New Harbinger Publications.

A nationally recognized speaker on women's special challenges with ADHD and the unique issues they face as parents when both they and their children have ADHD, Matlen has a passion for raising awareness about these topics. Her professional interests also include advocating for children with special needs.

Matlen says attending the various ADHD conventions and getting connected to other people with the disorder pushed her to grow. She is the former Vice President and a board member of ADDA and is a past Coordinator of East Oakland County CHADD (Michigan), currently serving on both professional advisory boards.

Matlen recalls, "The first time I attended an ADHD conference I felt like I was coming home. I had found my new family, my adult tribe in the ADD world. People there were forgetting each others' names, they were dropping things, losing things, but it was okay," she says with a laugh. "Finally I felt like I belonged. I was somewhere I could feel comfortable and safe."

Today Matlen loves helping others reach that point. For those recently diagnosed or still struggling, she says, "Don't go it alone."

"There are a lot of people out there who are just like you, looking to connect. You can find comfort and strength from connections, and you can learn new tools and strategies to live with this ADHD brain of yours."

"That doesn't mean my life is perfect," Matlen says, admitting to struggling with cooking, among other things. "I have still not conquered the kitchen, and entertaining is something I avoid. But I no longer let that say anything about *me*."

The clutter and paperwork haven't magically disappeared, either, but Matlen realizes those are lifelong challenges. "Sure, it can be frustrating, but it's not that I'm lazy or incompetent. I have all kinds of degrees that show otherwise. It's my biochemistry, and how is that any different from someone who has diabetes?"

She no longer focuses on her weaknesses, but chooses to concentrate on her strengths and all that she does well. She also makes time to do the things she loves—in particular, spending time in her music and art studios at home. "I have to," says Matlen, who plays five different instruments and writes songs (although finishes few). Raised in a home that always valued creativity and play, over time she has come to realize how much "creativity is a very important part of my life, and always has been."

Matlen also emphasizes the importance of acknowledging one's uniqueness, urging fellow ADDers to seek out therapists, coaches, counselors, and friends who understand them. "Get help, get support, read, study, and start looking at your strengths instead of your deficits. If you focus too much on your weaknesses, you are going to lose your authentic self."

GLOSSARY

<u>ADD/ADHD</u> – Attention Deficit Disorder/ Attention Deficit Hyperactivity Disorder. The latter is the official designation today, though many people still refer to the condition colloquially as ADD.

<u>ADDA (Attention Deficit Disorder Association)</u> – The world's leading adult ADHD organization, founded more than 20 years ago. ADDA brings together scientific perspectives and the human experience, providing information resources and networking opportunities to help adults with ADHD lead better lives. (Website: www.add.org)

<u>ADDCA (Attention Deficit Disorder Coach Academy)</u> – With a motto of "Launching ADHD Success," the goal of ADDCA is to prepare coaches with the foundational skills and understanding of the coaching profession as identified by the International Coach Federation. Coaches trained through ADDCA also learn what ADHD is, how it impacts every aspect of the ADDer's life, and how those with ADHD can learn tools and strategies to get on with their lives. (Website: www. addca.com)

<u>ADDers</u> – A term (often self-referential) for individuals living with ADHD.

<u>CHADD (Children and Adults with Attention-Deficit/Hyperactivity Disorder)</u> – A national, family-based organization concerned with ADHD and related disorders. CHADD hosts over 200 local chapters and community support groups. CHADD is active in Washington, DC, mental health and disability public policy coalitions, and is funded by the Centers for Disease Control and Prevention to operate the National Resource Center on ADHD. (Websites: www.chadd.org and www.help4adhd.org)

Judy Beth Brenis attended the ADD Coaching Academy, graduating the Basic ADHD Coach Training Program with an AAC designation. Prior to ADHD coaching, Judy earned a Bachelor's Degree in Journalism from Kent State University and has worked as a newspaper reporter and freelance writer for many years.

Judy's interest in ADHD began when her daughter—now twenty-four—received an ADHD diagnosis at age five. She is passionate about helping clients develop the tools and strategies to overcome challenges and acknowledge the hidden gifts ADHD brings.

Raised in Cleveland, Ohio, Judy moved to La Selva Beach, California, in 1985, where she found her special corner of the world.

Made in the USA
Lexington, KY
19 February 2014